Introduction To
LINE DESIGNS

by

Dale Seymour

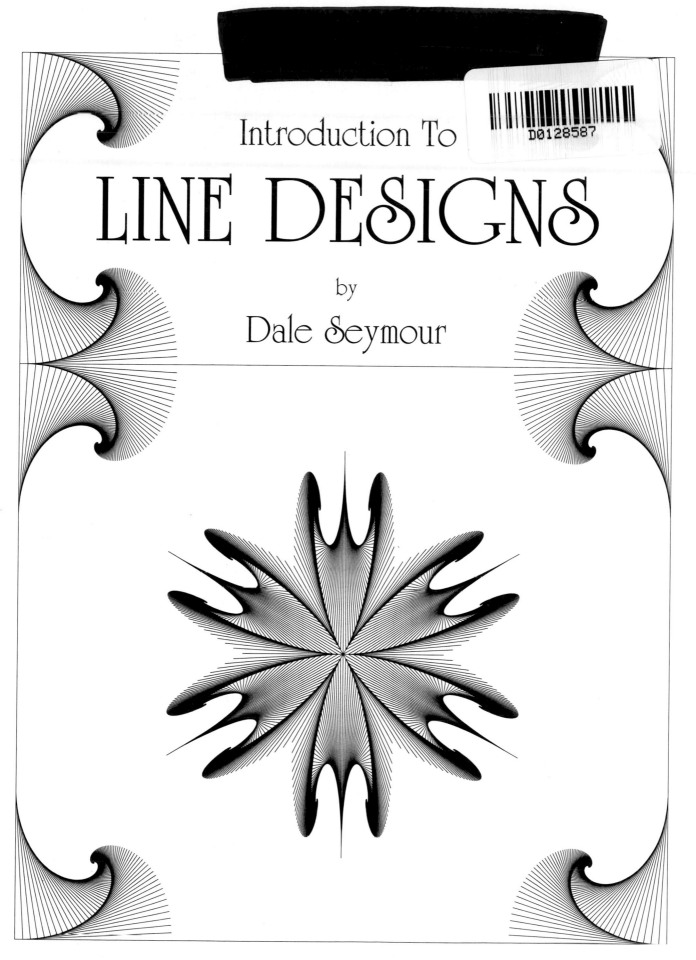

DALE SEYMOUR PUBLICATIONS

Dedication: I feel it most appropriate to dedicate this, my eightieth book, to my favorite octogenarians, Alice and Earl Seymour, my parents.

All illustrations in this book were drawn by the author on a Macintosh® IIfx with the Adobe Illustrator® 3.0 program.

ISBN 0-86651-579-8
Order Number DS21113

6 7 8 9 10 - MA - 99 98

DALE
SEYMOUR
PUBLICATIONS
P.O. BOX 10888
PALO ALTO, CA 94303

C
O
N
T
E
N
T
S

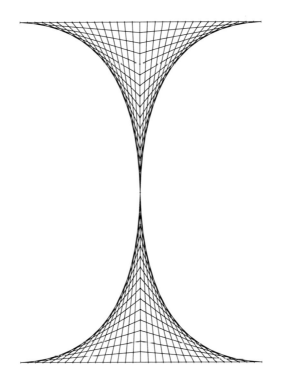

CHAPTER **1**

INTRODUCTION

Pattern as an element of design offers a certain fascination for many people. Pattern manifests itself in many ways through properties such as symmetry, repetition, translation, and illusion, to name a few. **Line designs**, the topic of this book, might be described as patterns that present illusions of curves. Most line designs are formed entirely by straight lines, yet they appear to contain or be formed by curves.

Exploring these geometrical shapes offers an opportunity to discover various properties of geometry as well as to exercize creative expression. The term *line design* is not well-defined, as are most mathematical words. The process of creating line designs is sometimes called *curve stitching* or *string art.* Line designs are created by performing a pattern of transformations on simple geometric elements. Figure 1-1, below, shows a simple 20° angle. The line design shown in Figure 1-2 has been created by making twenty-four 15° rotations of that angle. Figure 1-2 is made up entirely of straight lines; however, an illusion of a curve (circle) exists in the design.

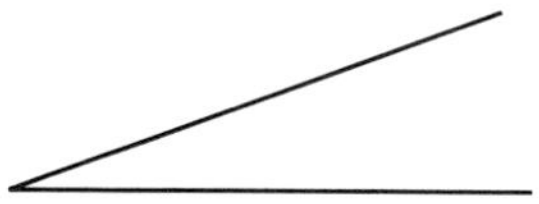

20° angle
Fig. 1-1

24 rotations of the angle
Fig. 1-2

Examples of line designs created by "fitting" line segments within the sides of an angle are shown below. Chapter 2 of this book will explain how this type of design is created. Chapter 3 will discuss how the designs can be made using a variety of different tools, such as pencils, pens, thread, and computers.

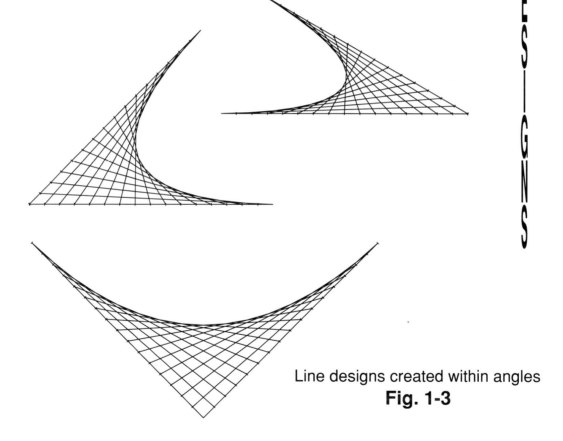

Line designs created within angles
Fig. 1-3

LINE DESIGNS

L
I
N
E
-
D
E
S
I
G
N
S

The curve illusions on the edges of the figures shown below are made by definite patterns. These curves have special mathematical properties, which are explained in chapter 11. It is not necessary to understand these properties to create the line designs themselves. It is interesting to some, however, to make these connections between mathematics and design.

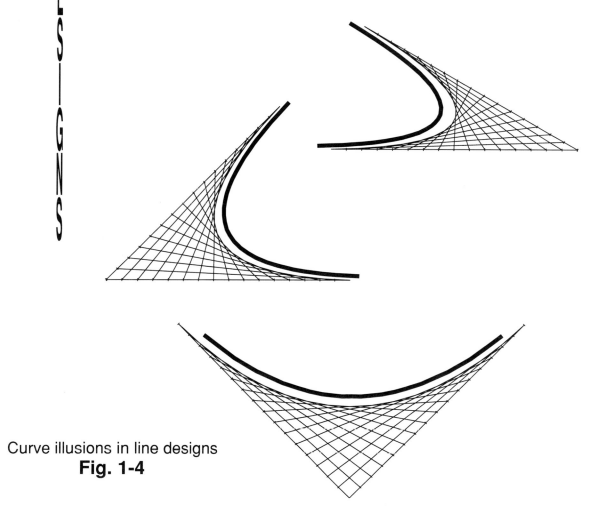

Curve illusions in line designs
Fig. 1-4

For many years, students of mathematics and art have exhibited their creativity and knowledge of elementary geometry with line design explorations. The first known publication on the subject was written in England in 1906 by Edith Somervell. Mrs. Somervell's classic book, *A Rhythmic Approach to Mathematics*, has been reprinted by The National Council of Teachers of Mathematics. It is interesting that Mrs. Somervell spends more time in the book proclaiming the virtues of this pastime than she does explaining how to create the designs. As seems to have been the trend around the turn of the century, she makes a case for this activity and her specific approach as providing a cure-all for many of education's shortcomings of that time. An example of her writing is shown as follows:

> *It is desirable to associate, in young children's minds, strict obedience to law with keen enjoyment of that sense of personal power given by finding an organic form growing under one's touch.*

> *The results obtained by a child, of exquisite curved and flower forms on the "back" of his card, by faithful obedience to a dull little rule in making straight stitches on the "front," is of the nature of a miracle. It should, therefore, be hardly necessary to insist that the less said the better, when the little worker produces anything especially beautiful or unexpected.*

Today, educators would say that students need hands-on involvement as opposed to an over-emphasis on memorization of geometric properties and relationships.

Attractive line design drawings can be made using only a ruler, pencil, and sheet of paper. Additional tools such as a compass and protractor enable one to create more sophisticated geometric shapes with pleasing symmetrical properties.

Because simple line designs require few prerequisite concepts or skills, they can be enjoyed by elementary grade students. At the same time, they offer a creative challenge to a professional designer. Personal computer drawing programs enable one to create elaborate designs in a fraction of the time it takes to do the same design with a pencil and straightedge. Chapter 3 addresses the use of computer drawing programs.

Some of the relationships explored or generated in the creation of a design may reveal some advanced math concepts. Shapes such as ellipses, parabolas, and hyperbolas may be interesting to those who have studied them, but they are not prerequisite to creating designs that reveal them. Chapter 11 introduces some of these curves for those who are interested. This book is designed as a simple introduction to line designs for a broad audience.

Teachers may wish to offer their art or math students a brief introduction to the curves that are involved. Students who are highly motivated by creating line designs willingly spend hours on their own time exploring and expressing their creativity. Line design projects are among the most common projects chosen by students for math fairs. This book may serve as a resource for students undertaking such a project.

The author has found that his students were able to make more sophisticated designs and understand their composure when the line design activities were preceded by a unit on geometric constructions.

This book concentrates on two-dimensional line designs. The techniques presented in creating designs in a plane can be extended to create beautiful 3-D sculptures as well. One's own imagination is the only limiting factor when exploring the vast realm of design possibilities.

A bibliography is provided in the back of the book for those wishing to further investigate other designs or concepts. The author would enjoy receiving copies of your creative endeavors or other comments about this fascinating topic.

LINE DESIGNS

CHAPTER 2

CURVES FROM
SEGMENTS IN
AN ANGLE

The most commonly used technique for creating a line design is to divide both sides of an angle into an equal number of equal parts. These dividing points are then connected by line segments, which ultimately appear to outline a curve.

Figures 2-1 through 2-6 show the simple step-by-step procedures for creating a line design within an angle. Sides are first divided into an equal number of parts. The division point closest to the angle vertex on one side of the angle is connected with the last division point on the other angle side. Next, the second closest division to the vertex is connected to the second farthest division, the third closest to the third farthest, and so on. All lines connecting the points are straight line segments.

Step-by-Step Creation of a
Line Design in an Angle

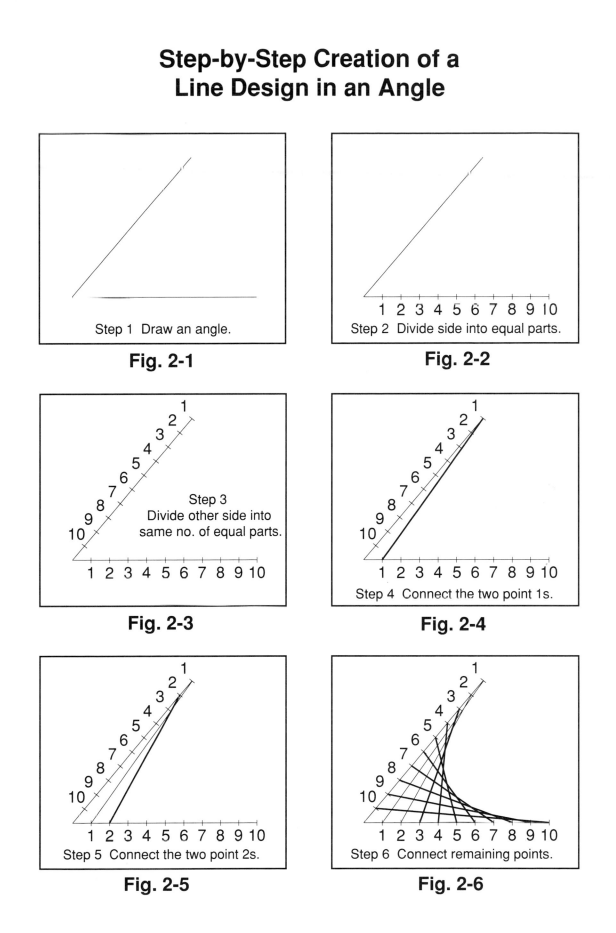

Step 1 Draw an angle.

Fig. 2-1

Step 2 Divide side into equal parts.

Fig. 2-2

Step 3
Divide other side into
same no. of equal parts.

Fig. 2-3

Step 4 Connect the two point 1s.

Fig. 2-4

Step 5 Connect the two point 2s.

Fig. 2-5

Step 6 Connect remaining points.

Fig. 2-6

When all the corresponding division points are connected, the line design is completed. Notice how the combination of these "shifted" segments combine to form the illusion of a curve. Yet, no curve was drawn. All the segments drawn were straight lines.

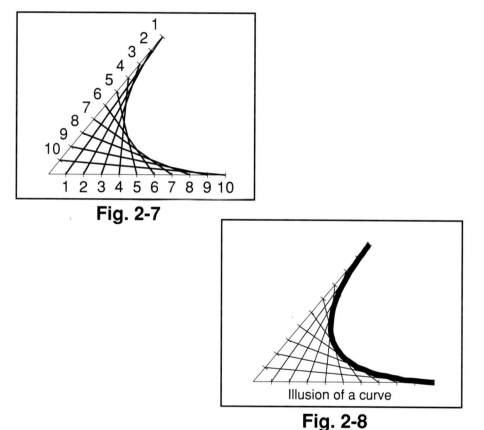

Fig. 2-7

Illusion of a curve

Fig. 2-8

This same process can be used with any size angle and still produce the curve illusion. The opposite page shows examples of a variety of angle bases for line designs.

Line Designs Formed in Various Angle Sizes

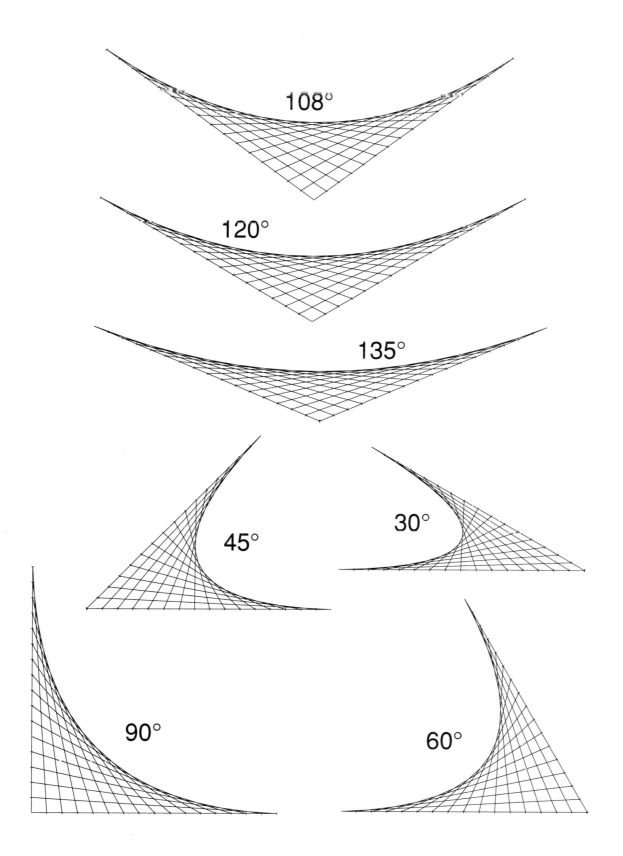

Angle sides that form the line designs can be divided into any number of divisions that are practical. Too few divisions may result in a design that produces less of an angle illusion. Too many divisions may prove to be too time consuming or produce lines that are too congested. Usually between 12 and 24 divisions is most desirable.

Several examples are shown in the figure on the opposite page.

LINE DESIGNS

Examples of Various Angle Side Divisions

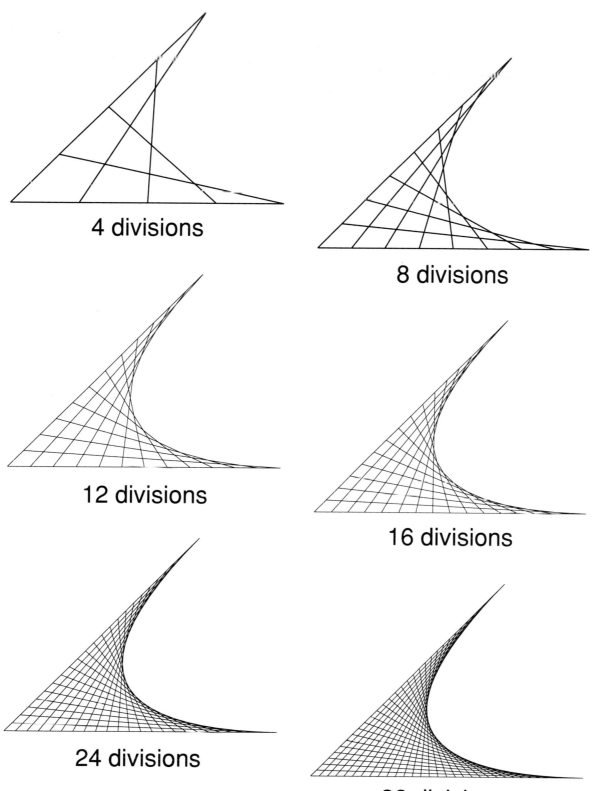

4 divisions

8 divisions

12 divisions

16 divisions

24 divisions

32 divisions

Whether the lines of the design are formed by pencil, pen, thread, string, or computer is up to the designer. Each of these approaches will be addressed in some detail in later chapters. The width of the line in proportion to its length can produce varying effects.

Examples are shown on the opposite page.

LINE DESIGNS

Examples of Various Line Widths

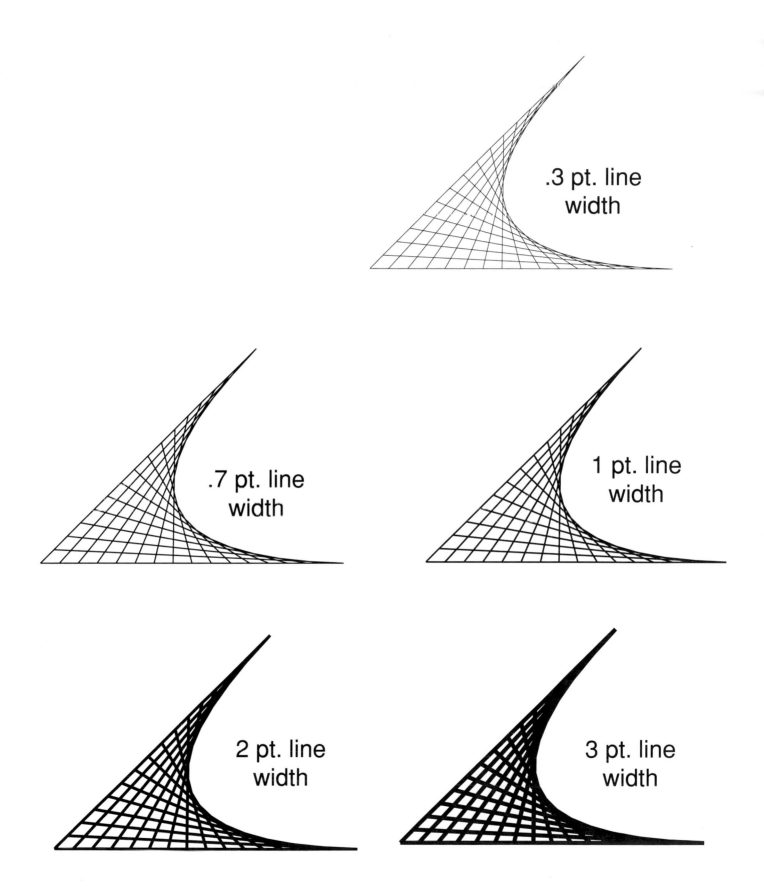

.3 pt. line width

.7 pt. line width

1 pt. line width

2 pt. line width

3 pt. line width

Professional artists and illustrators use drawing pens that produce various-sized line widths. These pens are readily available at most art supply stores or stationery stores. The designs on the opposite page are examples of the different effects that line width can have on a drawing.

LINE DESIGNS

Examples of Various Line Widths

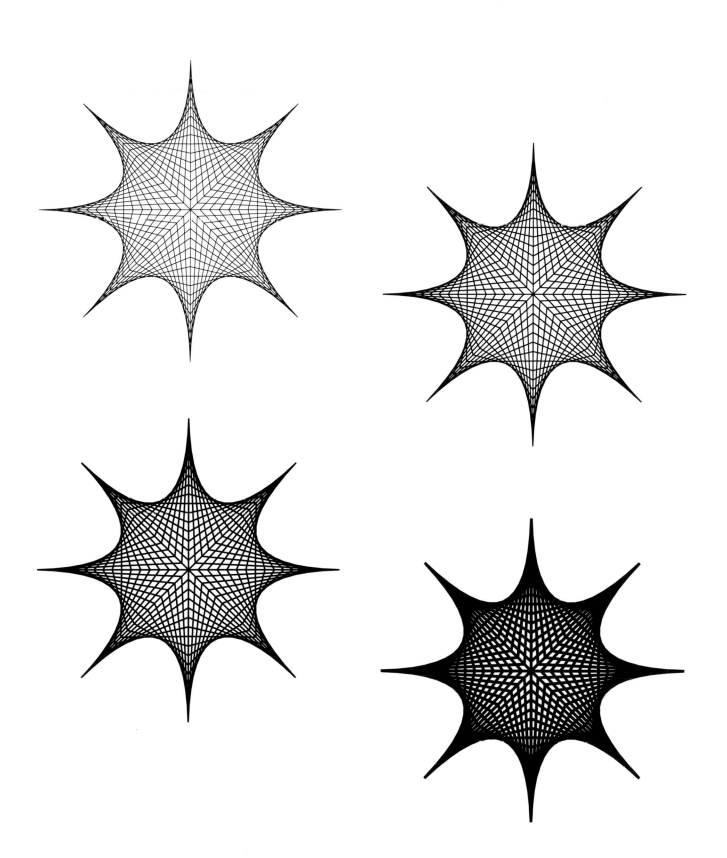

The two rays that form the sides of an angle can be any length. In all the examples shown thus far in this book, both sides of all angles have been the same measure. Line designs can be formed within angles whose side lengths differ, also. It is important, however, that (1) the side lengths of the angle are each divided into the same number of divisions and (2) each side is divided into equal segments.

The figures on the opposite page show the steps in drawing a line design within an angle whose side lengths differ.

LINE DESIGNS

Step-by-Step Creation of a Line Design in an Angle with Sides of Different Lengths

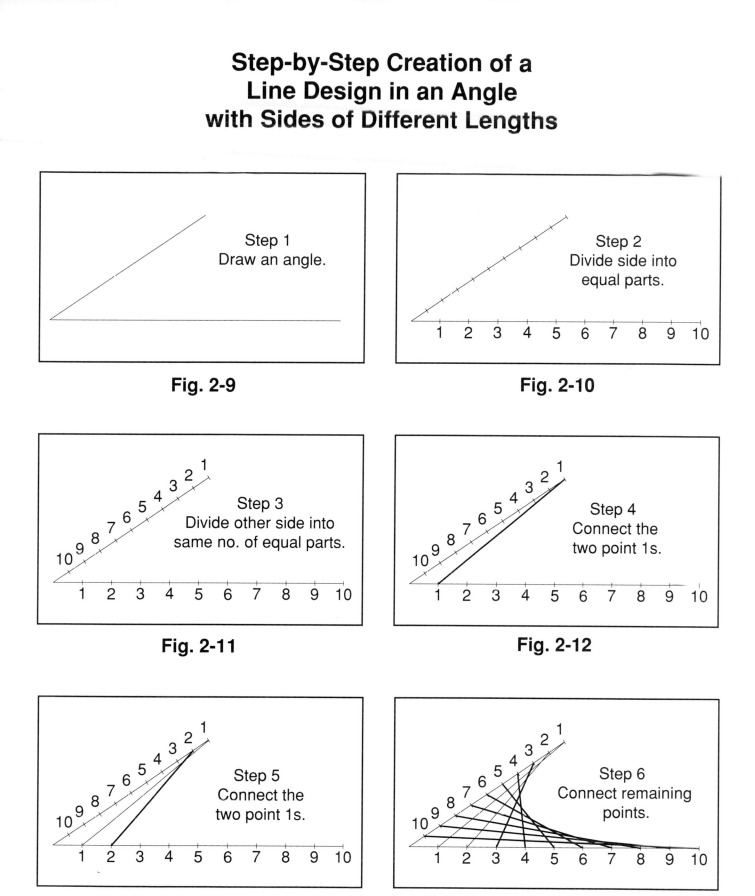

Step 1
Draw an angle.

Fig. 2-9

Step 2
Divide side into equal parts.

Fig. 2-10

Step 3
Divide other side into same no. of equal parts.

Fig. 2-11

Step 4
Connect the two point 1s.

Fig. 2-12

Step 5
Connect the two point 1s.

Fig. 2-13

Step 6
Connect remaining points.

Fig. 2-14

Additional examples of line designs formed within angles with different length divisions are shown on the opposite page. Notice that the smooth curve illusion remains.

LINE DESIGNS

Examples of Line Designs
with Sides of
Different Lengths

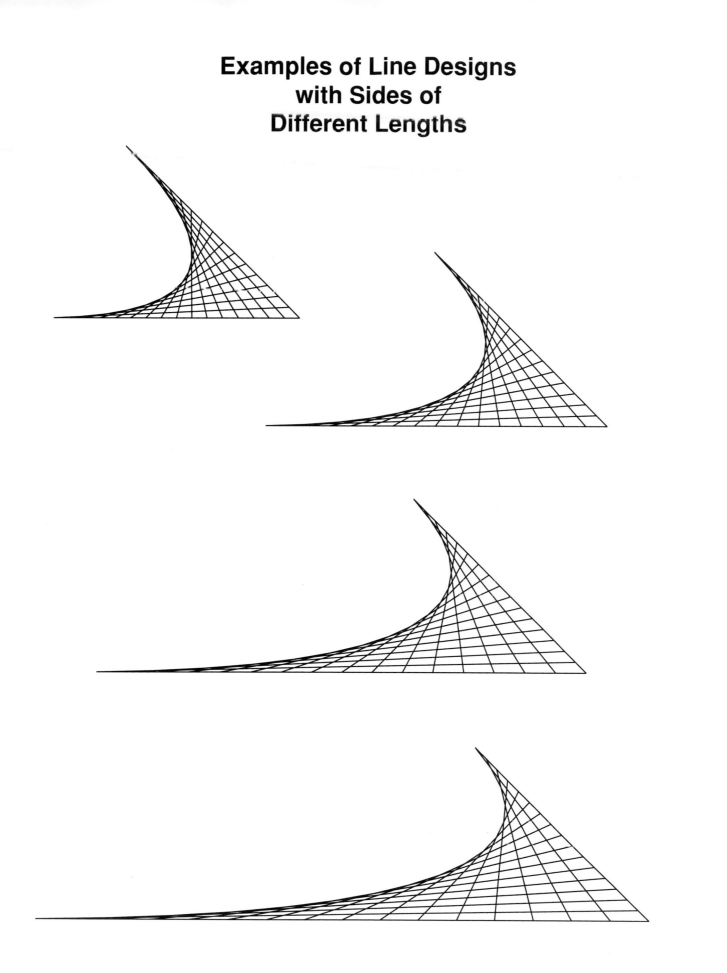

A line design created within one angle may be interesting but not necessarily beautiful. Line design angles can serve as the "building blocks" for more interesting designs by combining two or more angles. When angles share a common side they are called adjacent angles. Adjacent angle designs make line designs more complex and interesting.

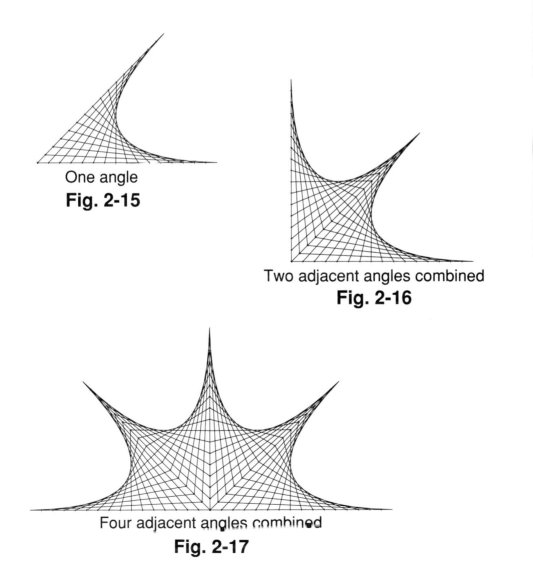

One angle
Fig. 2-15

Two adjacent angles combined
Fig. 2-16

Four adjacent angles combined
Fig. 2-17

LINE DESIGNS

Angles need not be equal in measure in order to combine them to form interesting designs. It is, however, most often interesting to have the common sides of adjacent angles have equal divisions and the same number of divisions. Various combinations are shown below.

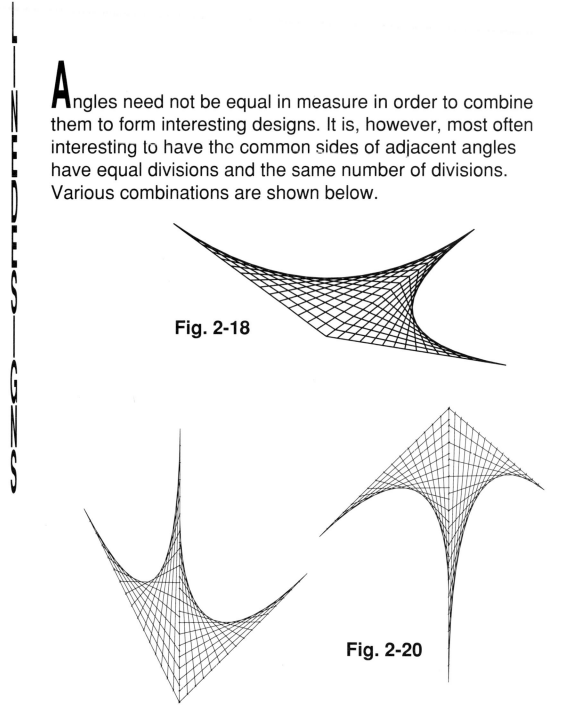

Fig. 2-18

Fig. 2-20

Fig. 2-19

Often designs appear more pleasing if they are "whole." That is, if they completely surround a point in a plane or if they contain rotational or mirror symmetry. Combinations of angles that form a total of 360° might be referred to as "compatible angles." Four squares or six equilateral triangles are examples of compatible angles.

The next several pages show examples of designs created from various selections of angles in squares and hexagons. Observe the many options one has in choosing combinations of angles.

Examples of Designs from Combined Angles

FOUR SQUARES ➡	ANGLE CHOICE ➡	FINAL DESIGN

A Design from Combined Angles

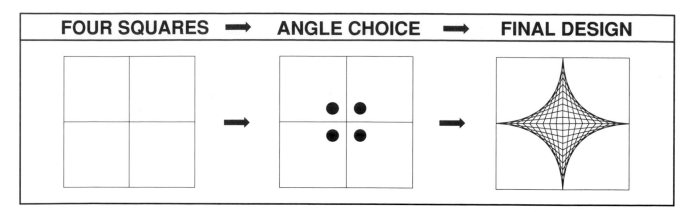

FOUR SQUARES	ANGLE CHOICE	FINAL DESIGN

A Design from Joining Several Square Designs

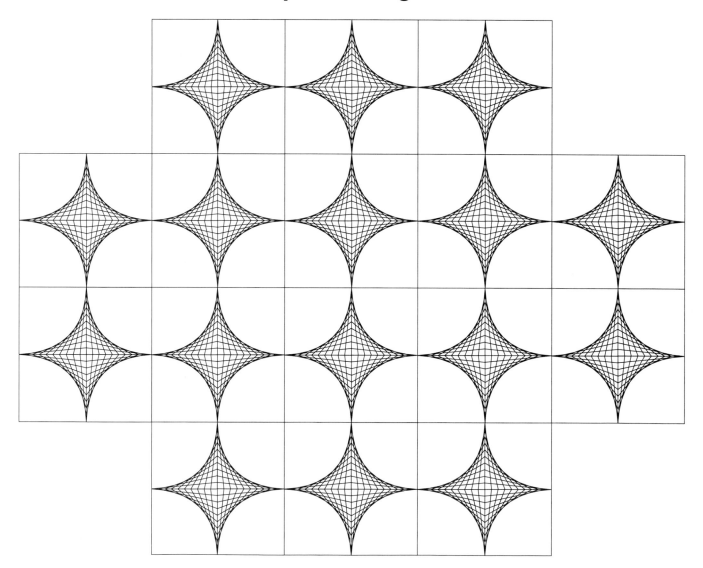

A Design from Combined Angles

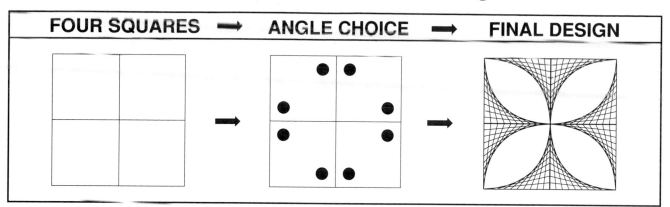

FOUR SQUARES ➡	ANGLE CHOICE ➡	FINAL DESIGN

A Design from Joining Several Square Designs

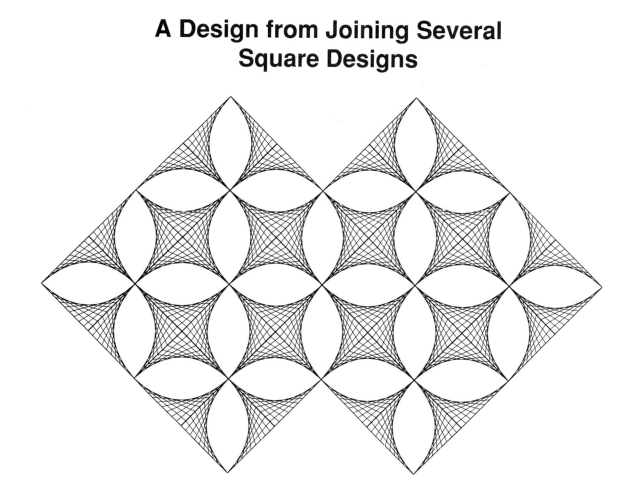

A Design from Combined Angles

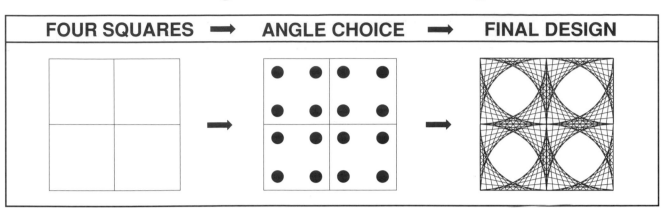

FOUR SQUARES	⟶	ANGLE CHOICE	⟶	FINAL DESIGN

A Design from Joining Several Square Designs

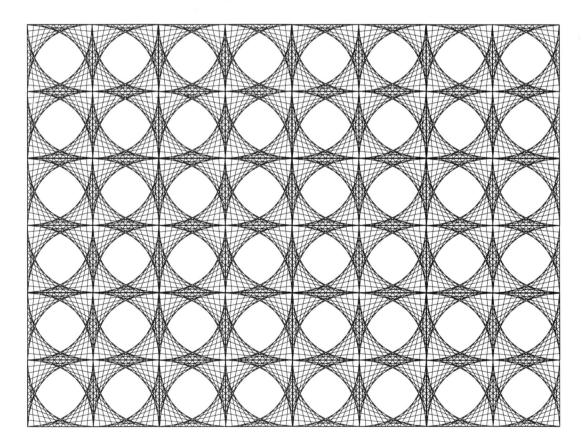

Examples of Designs from Combined Angles

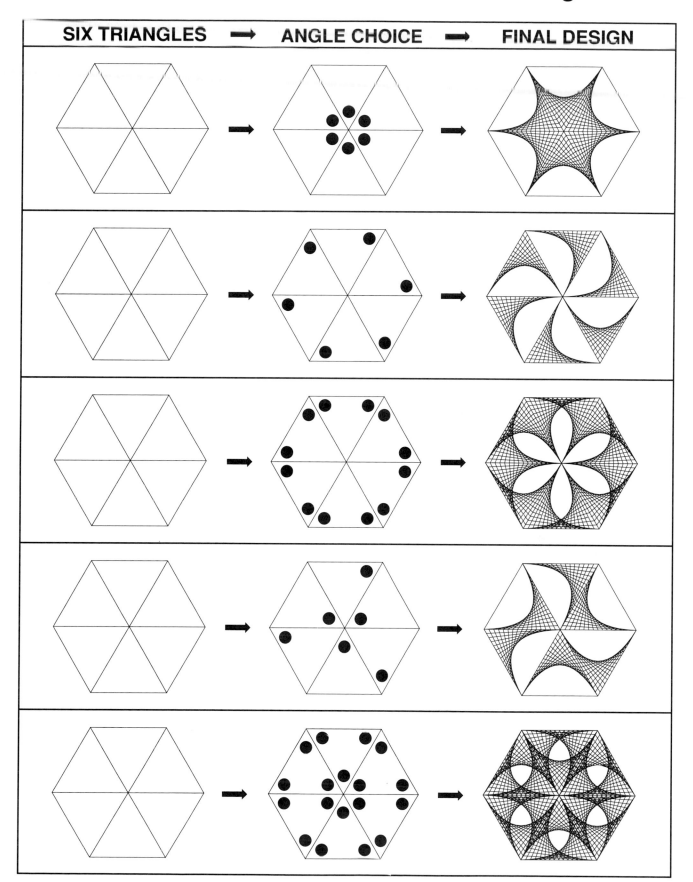

SIX TRIANGLES →	ANGLE CHOICE →	FINAL DESIGN

A Design from Combined Angles

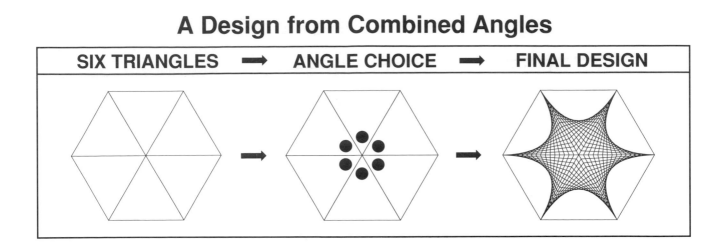

SIX TRIANGLES	⟹	ANGLE CHOICE	⟹	FINAL DESIGN

A Design from Joining Several Hexagon Designs

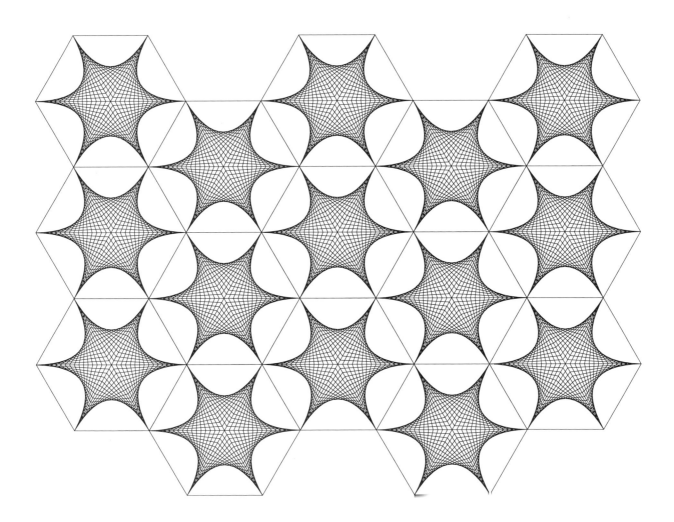

A Design from Combined Angles

SIX TRIANGLES ➡	ANGLE CHOICE ➡	FINAL DESIGN

A Design from Joining Several Hexagon Designs

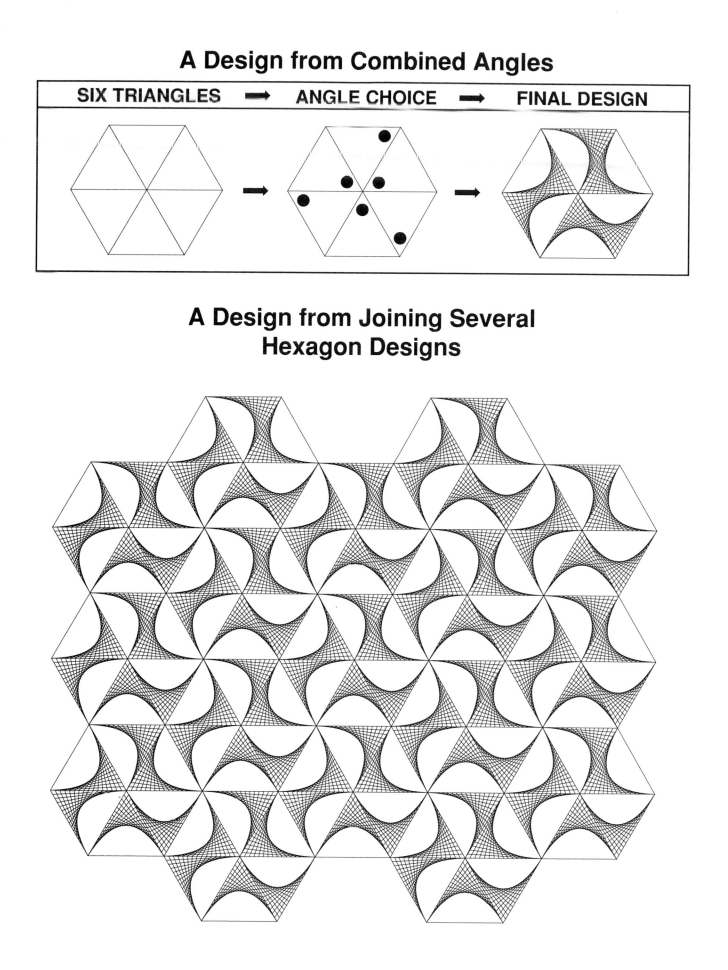

A Design from Combined Angles

SIX TRIANGLES ➡	ANGLE CHOICE ➡	FINAL DESIGN

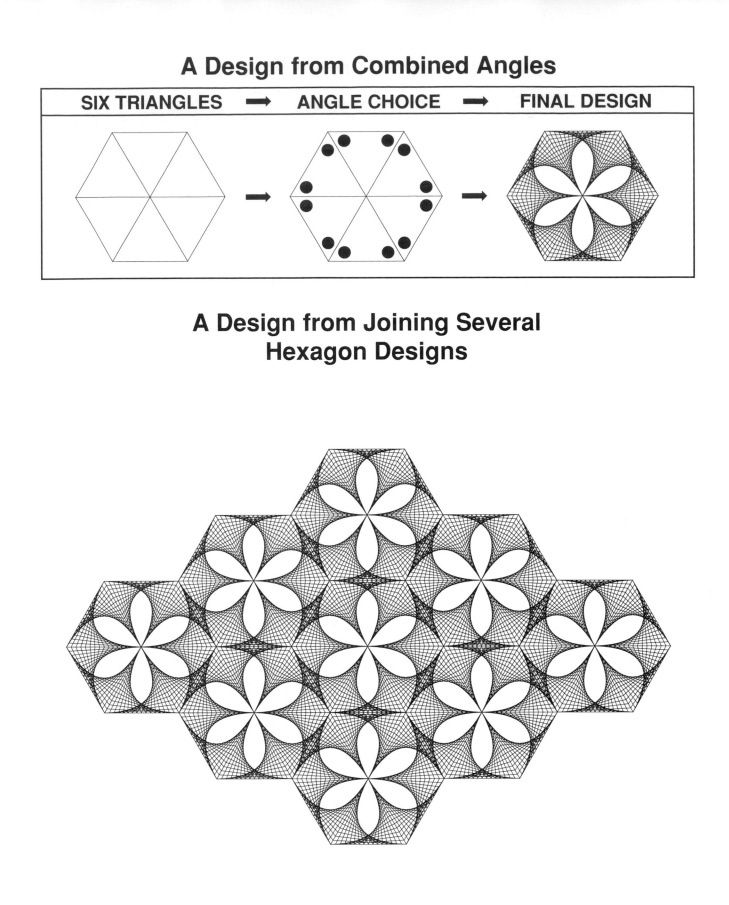

A Design from Joining Several Hexagon Designs

A Design from Combined Angles

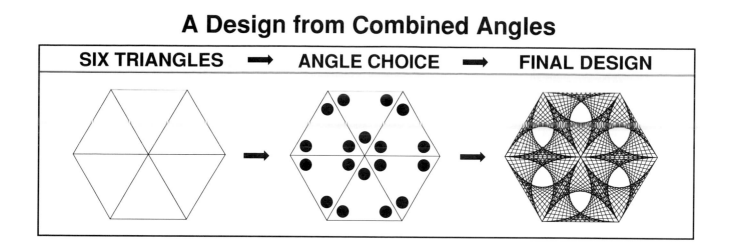

SIX TRIANGLES	➡	ANGLE CHOICE	➡	FINAL DESIGN

A Design from Joining Several Hexagon Designs

As you can see from examples in the past few pages, some line design angles overlap each other. Overlapping design can create interesting effects. Chapter 7 will address these designs in greater detail.

Just as an angle can be used as a building block to create more complex designs, polygon designs can be used in combination. Polygon shapes that cover all of a plane in a pattern without any gaps or overlaps are said to *tessellate.* Any triangle or quadrilateral will tessellate a plane by itself. The opposite page shows a design created from tessellating hexagons. The following two pages show designs possibilities from tessellating triangles and quadrilaterals.

LINE DESIGNS

Three Designs from Combined Angles

A Design from Joining Different Hexagon Designs

An Example of Tessellating Triangles

Line Design in Smallest Angle of Same Triangles

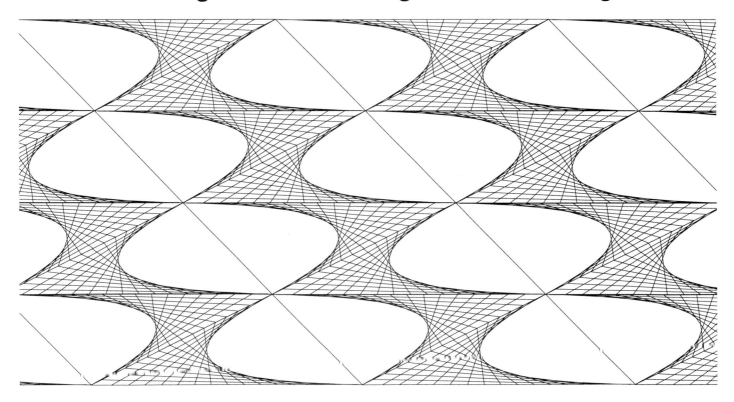

An Example of Tessellating Quadrilaterals

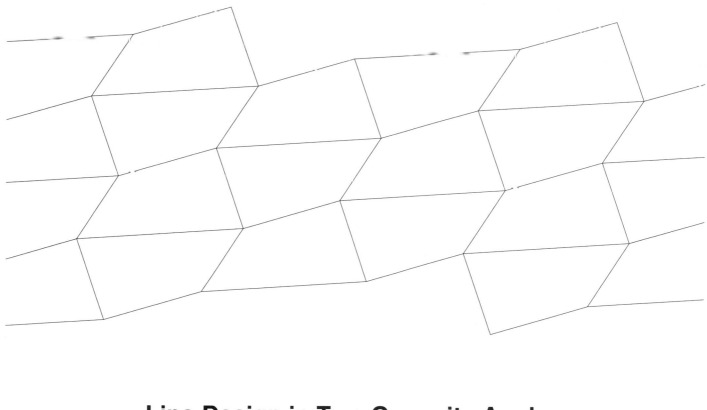

Line Design in Two Opposite Angles

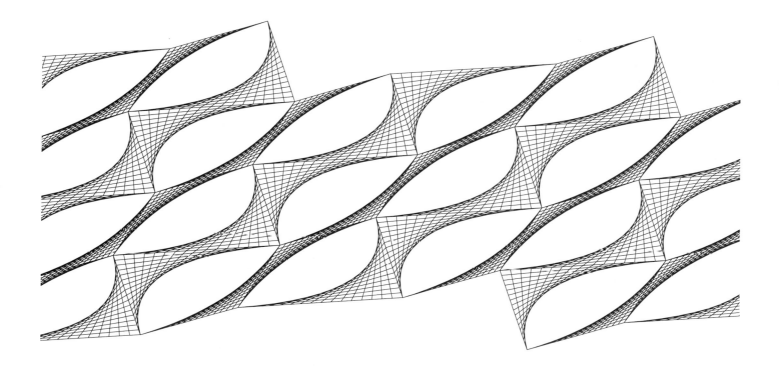

In order for a designer to make the most interesting and beautiful designs, it may be helpful to be able to draw, construct, or create certain special angle sizes and polygonal shapes. In some order of importance, these angle sizes are arguably: 90°, 60°, 30°, 120°, 45°, 72°, 108°, 135°, etc. A designer has the choice of creating angles with a protractor, compass, template, or computer. In certain circumstances, one tool may be faster or more accurate. Ideally, one who knows how to use all these tools can choose the appropriate tool for the special design requirement involved.

Regular polygons are the basis for many interesting designs. It is helpful to know or be able to calculate the angle measures and central angles of regular polygons. A classroom unit on creating line designs is much richer if preceded by some instruction on geometric construction.

A chart of selected regular polygon relationships is shown on the opposite page.

Selected Regular Polygons
and Angle Measures

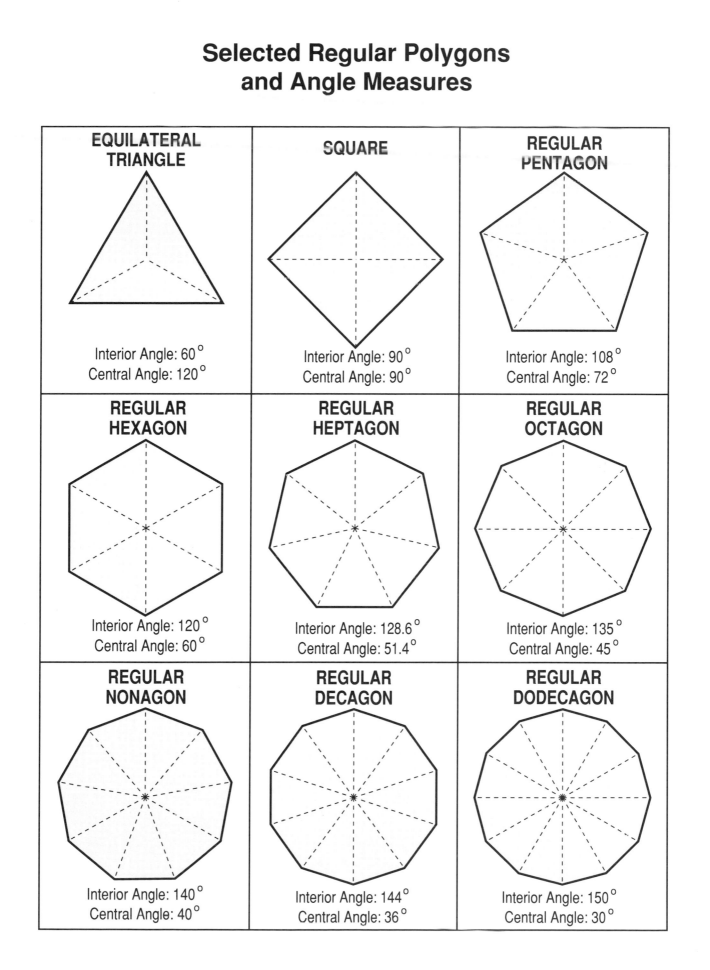

EQUILATERAL TRIANGLE

Interior Angle: 60°
Central Angle: 120°

SQUARE

Interior Angle: 90°
Central Angle: 90°

REGULAR PENTAGON

Interior Angle: 108°
Central Angle: 72°

REGULAR HEXAGON

Interior Angle: 120°
Central Angle: 60°

REGULAR HEPTAGON

Interior Angle: 128.6°
Central Angle: 51.4°

REGULAR OCTAGON

Interior Angle: 135°
Central Angle: 45°

REGULAR NONAGON

Interior Angle: 140°
Central Angle: 40°

REGULAR DECAGON

Interior Angle: 144°
Central Angle: 36°

REGULAR DODECAGON

Interior Angle: 150°
Central Angle: 30°

CHAPTER **3**

PENCIL, THREAD, STRING, OR COMPUTER?

Line designs can be created in a variety of ways. They can be drawn with pencil or pen, sewn with thread, wrapped with string, or constructed on a computer screen. Each of these methods has advantages and disadvantages. This chapter will address all of these options in some detail. Naturally, factors such as availability of tools and materials, manual dexterity, artistic experience, and knowledge of geometry will probably determine the choice for creating designs.

Pencil and Pen Drawings

Teachers have had success with young primary students creating designs with only a pencil and ruler. At higher levels, students often start drawing their first designs with pencil, then are given a choice of doing their "final" design in colored pens or thread.

If soft-lead pencils are used, the final drawing is often smudged with graphite from the pencil. When working with young students it is advisable to take time initially to see that pencils are sharp, lead is hard, rulers are straight, and hands are clean. Often the initial pencil drawing is just a preliminary step to determine the line positions for inking or the hole positions for sewing.

Students may have more difficulty avoiding smudges with an ink pen than they do with a pencil. Ask them to test their pens thoroughly on scratch paper before they embark on a final inking. It is important that they know how long it takes for the ink to dry and what kinds of pressure create smears.

Ballpoint pens have a tendency to smear because their ink does not dry rapidly. Permanent felt-tip pens are better for making final drawings. Professional drawing pens with various line widths are available at art supply stores. Inking can be done directly over pencil lines. A good quality art gum eraser will remove all signs of pencil marks after the ink has dried. If a compass is used to mark off equal segments or to construct a basic underlying figure, the holes left by the compass can detract from the appearance of the drawing. These holes can be avoid by tracing the final drawing points onto a clean sheet of paper or by having a hard surface beneath the compass point so as not to leave a sizable hole in the paper.

One's first line design drawing is usually created within an acute angle. First, the angle is drawn, then the sides are divided into an equal number of parts. Next, the division points are connected as described in the previous chapter. Equal segments can be marked off with a ruler or a compass. It is much easier to mark off equal segments on an angle side of arbitrary length than it is to divide a given line length into equal parts. The line-divider device pictured in Fig. 3-1 can be used to divide a segment into equal parts.

The line divider is meant to be photocopied and used as a separate sheet of paper. Horizontally, its segments are divided into 20 equal divisions. The line divider may be used to divide any line less than 6 inches into 20 or fewer equal segments.

To use the line divider, first tape it to a window or place it on a light table. The light source is needed to make the line divider's lines visible through your line to be divided. Next, determine how many divisions you want for your segment. Place the segment to be divided on top of the line divider, lining up the left end of the segment with the

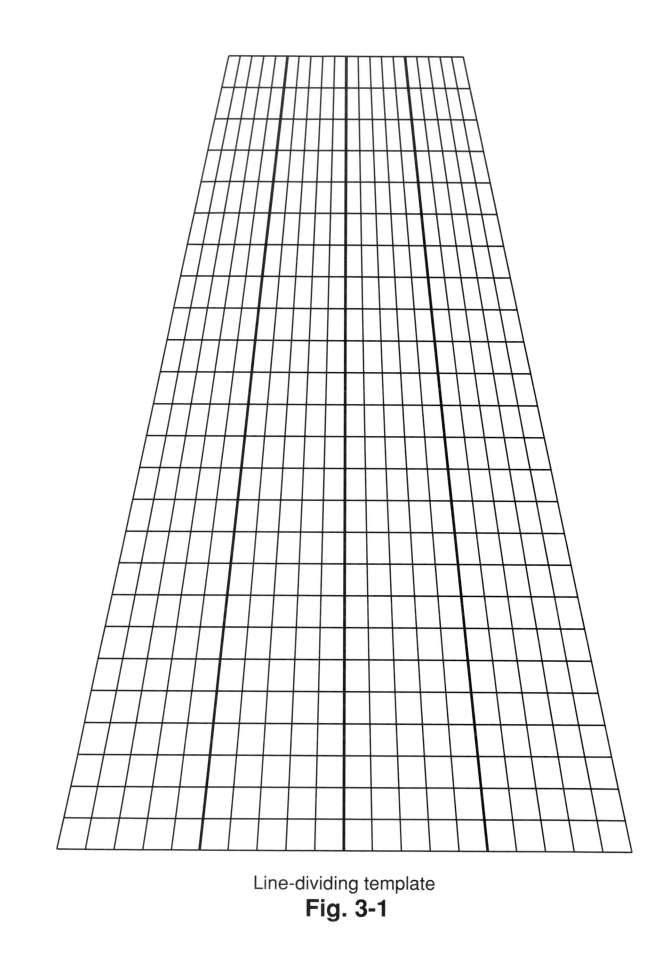

Line-dividing template

Fig. 3-1

upper left end of the line divider. Slide the sheet of paper containing the segment to be divided down over the line divider until the right end of the segment coincides with the mark designating the number of units desired. Finally, mark off the units on your segment.

The figures below show how a segment (*AB*) can be divided into 16 equal segments.

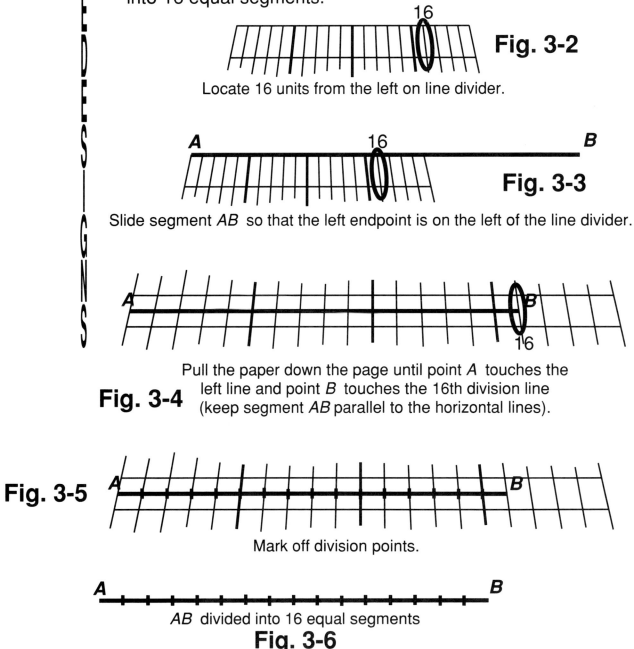

16

Locate 16 units from the left on line divider.

Fig. 3-2

A   16   *B*

Slide segment *AB* so that the left endpoint is on the left of the line divider.

Fig. 3-3

A   *B*
16

Pull the paper down the page until point *A* touches the left line and point *B* touches the 16th division line (keep segment *AB* parallel to the horizontal lines).

Fig. 3-4

Fig. 3-5

A   *B*

Mark off division points.

A —————————————— *B*

AB divided into 16 equal segments

Fig. 3-6

The nine illustrations on this page and the next show a step-by-step procedure for constructing a geometric shape, creating a line design, inking the design, and, finally, erasing the pencil marks.

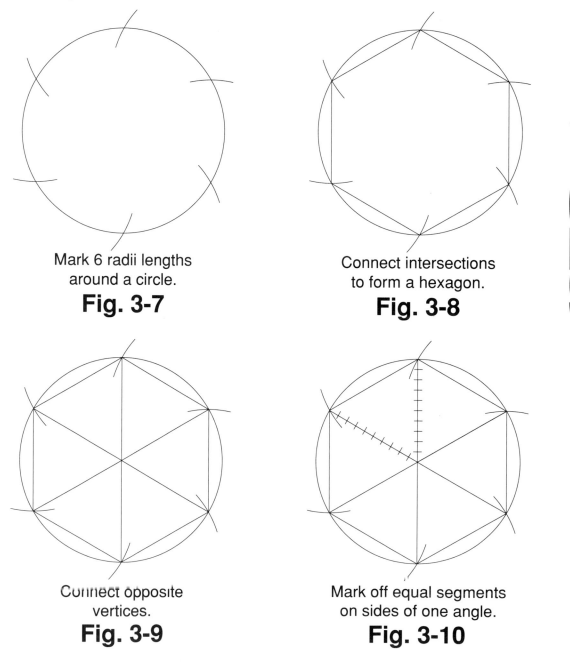

Mark 6 radii lengths
around a circle.
Fig. 3-7

Connect intersections
to form a hexagon.
Fig. 3-8

Connect opposite
vertices.
Fig. 3-9

Mark off equal segments
on sides of one angle.
Fig. 3-10

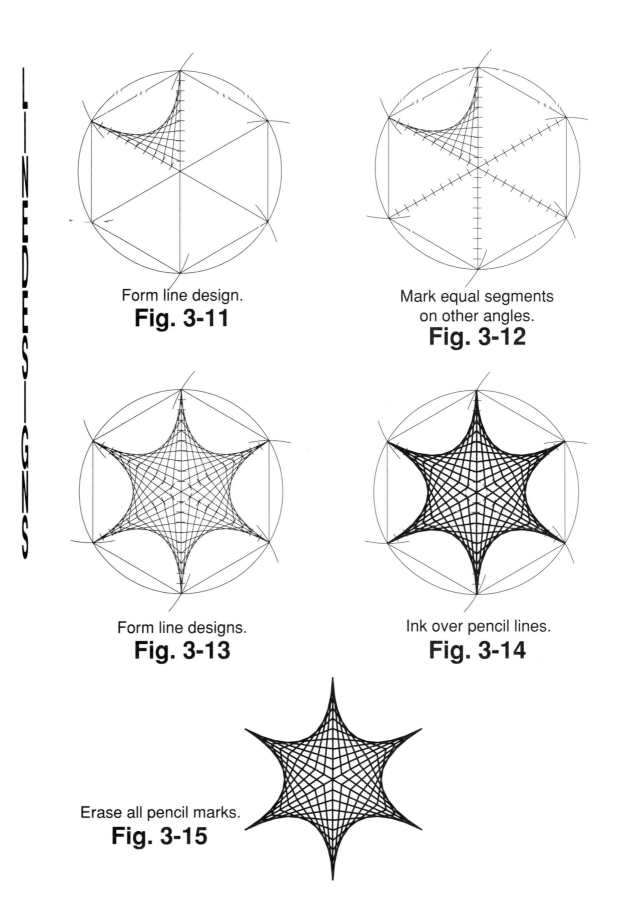

LINE DESIGNS

Form line design.
Fig. 3-11

Mark equal segments
on other angles.
Fig. 3-12

Form line designs.
Fig. 3-13

Ink over pencil lines.
Fig. 3-14

Erase all pencil marks.
Fig. 3-15

Sewing with Thread, String, or Yarn

Line designs created with colored thread can produce attractive wall hangings. Thread has the advantage over ink of being available in a multitude of colors. Thread also can be selected in various thicknesses and sheens. And thread will not smear like pencil and ink drawings. On the other hand, a broken thread can destroy the appearance of a design.

In a thread design, threads are stretched tight from hole to hole to form the straight lines of the design. The background material must be sturdy enough so that tightly pulled thread will not bend the surface of the background. Poster board or tagboard is advisable to ensure the necessary rigidity. The initial design can be drawn on regular paper and then placed over the tagboard where the holes for threading are punched through both the paper and the tagboard.

Procedures for creating the "curve stitching" are quite similar to making pencil and ink designs. First, a design is chosen and created with a pencil, straightedge, and compass. Next, line divisions of angle sides are marked. When the pencil drawing is completed, that paper is mounted to the rigid tagboard surface. Use a push pin, compass point, or needle to punch the holes at the end of each line segment in the drawing. Make the holes as small as possible so that they will not be obvious in the final result.

When all the holes have been punched, the original pencil lines can be erased if you will bo throading over that paper.

If not, discard the design paper with the pencil marks. The underneath surface will contain all the holes that are needed to make the design.

Once the holes are all punched, the needle is threaded and the straight lines that form the design are stitched. Lines are stitched just as the straight lines were drawn in the pencil drawing Begin by using a thread line of 2–3 feet. It is not necessary to have all the thread for the entire drawing on the needle when you begin. Tape the end of the thread to the back side of the tagboard near the hole where you choose to begin threading. Push the threaded needle through the hole (line segment endpoint), coming out the front side. Find the hole at the end of that line segment and push the needle through that hole to the back side. Pull the thread tight so that you have a nice straight line on the front of your design. Find the hole that represents the end of the next line you wish to stitch. Push the needle through from the back side and continue to stitch each line segment that you wish to show in the drawing.

Remember that the back side appearance is not that important, but keep the thread tight on both the front and back sides. You may wish to tape over the threads in the back from time to time. This will help ensure that the threads stay tight. It is always a good idea to experiment with a very simple design first, just for practice. It is equally important to experiment with the tagboard you choose just to be sure it has the required stability. When the final design has been made, you may wish to cover all the threads in the back by gluing on another piece of tagboard. This will protect the threads from being cut and also hide the unattractive back side.

Drawing Line Designs with a Computer

There are currently several computer software drawing programs on the market that can be used to create beautiful line designs. These programs include Adobe Illustrator®, Aldus Freehand™, MacDraw®, MacDraft®, and Canvas™. Creating a design on a personal computer is significantly faster and more accurate than doing it by hand. The problem-solving challenges of how to create the underlying design or pattern still remain in the computer approach. The tedious, time-consuming repetition required in some designs is often eliminated or greatly reduce when using the computer. A good computer drawing program enables one to change such elements of a drawing as the line widths. If a design is created with a given line width, in a matter of seconds that same design can be viewed in several different line widths to see which is most pleasing.

Drawing programs offer tools such as translation (slide), rotation (turn), reflection (flip), enlargement, and reduction. Other tools such as shear and blend offer creative explorations. The laser printer allows designs to be printed from the computer in a commercial quality. Designs can also be transferred on a disk to be printed by high-resolution linotronic printers. With today's modern technology, beautiful, detailed design capability is easily accessible. All the designs in this book were created by the author on a Macintosh® IIfx with the Adobe Illustrator® 3.0.1 software.

Three-Dimensional Line Designs

This book addresses only two-dimensional designs drawn
on a plane surface. Most of the basic ideas presented in
the book can be extended into three dimensions. These
designs might take the shape of cubes, cylinders, spheres,
or polyhedra. Adding a dimension takes the design into
the realm of artistic sculptures. Lines in three dimensions
would be represented by thread, string, yarn, wire, or cable,
while surfaces might be cardboard, wood, Plexiglas™ or
ceramic. Line designs made in three dimensions offer a
fertile ground for creativity and demonstration of numerous
mathematical properties and patterns.

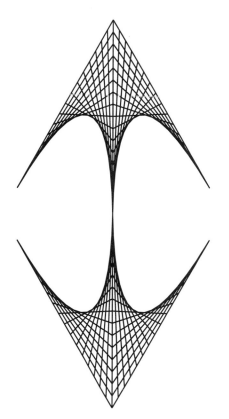

4

DESIGNS FROM
COMBINED ANGLES

Several types of line designs are shown in this chapter. There are representative examples of each type of design explained in Chapter 2.

Studying designs and analyzing how they might be created will provide ideas for creating your own original designs. The design on the opposite page, for example, was created from three 120° angles.

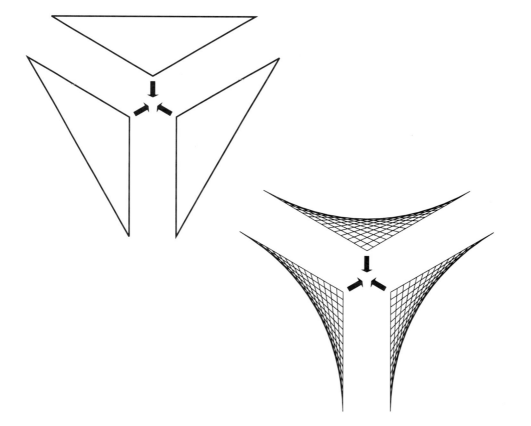

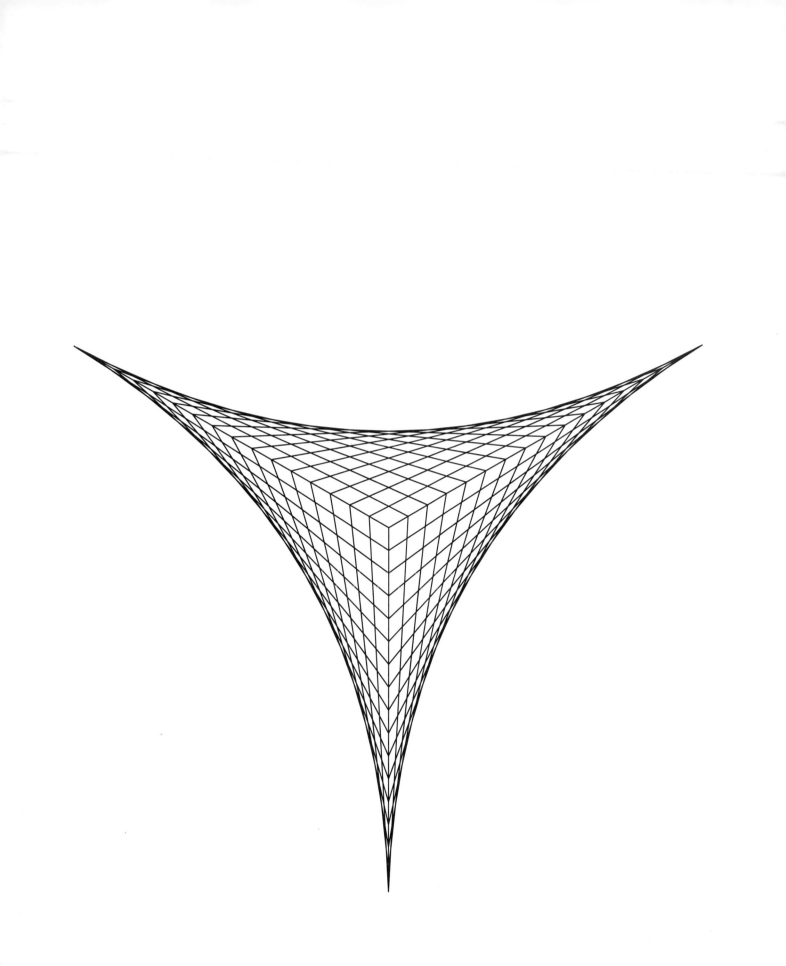

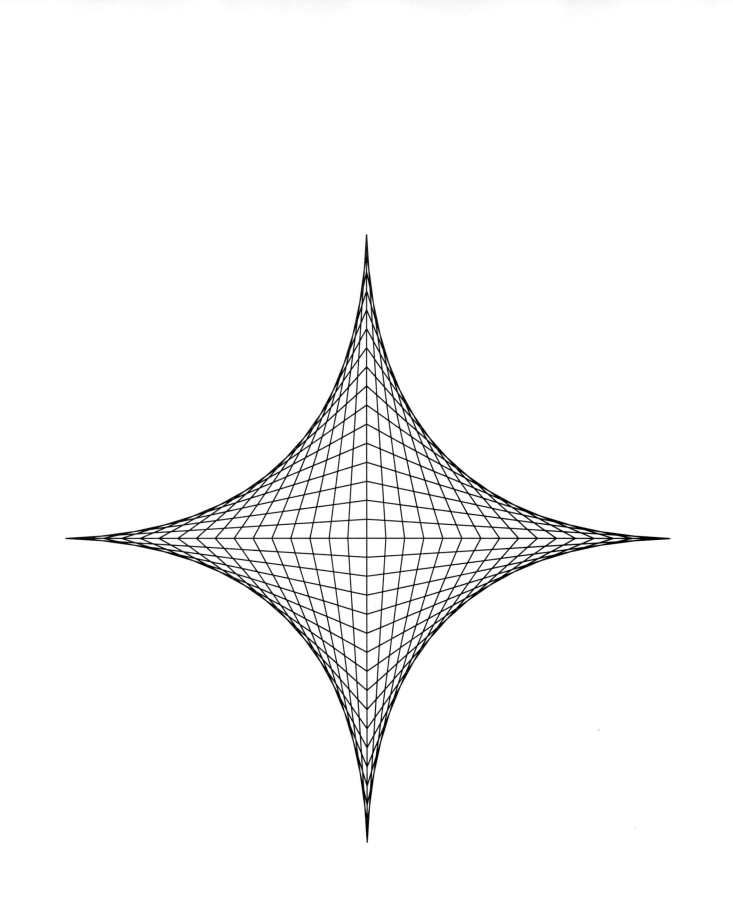

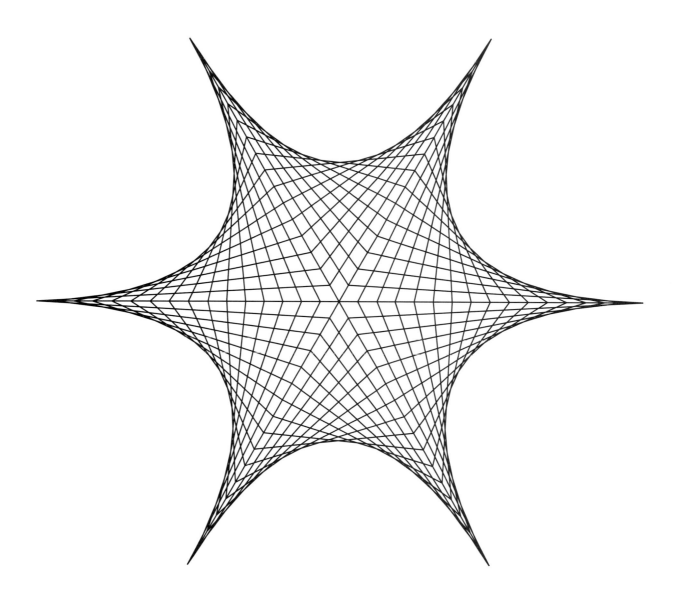

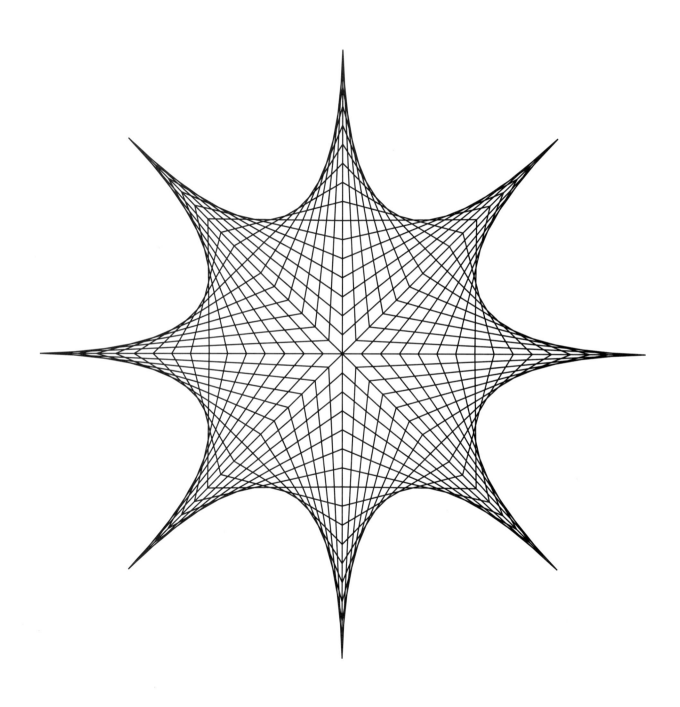

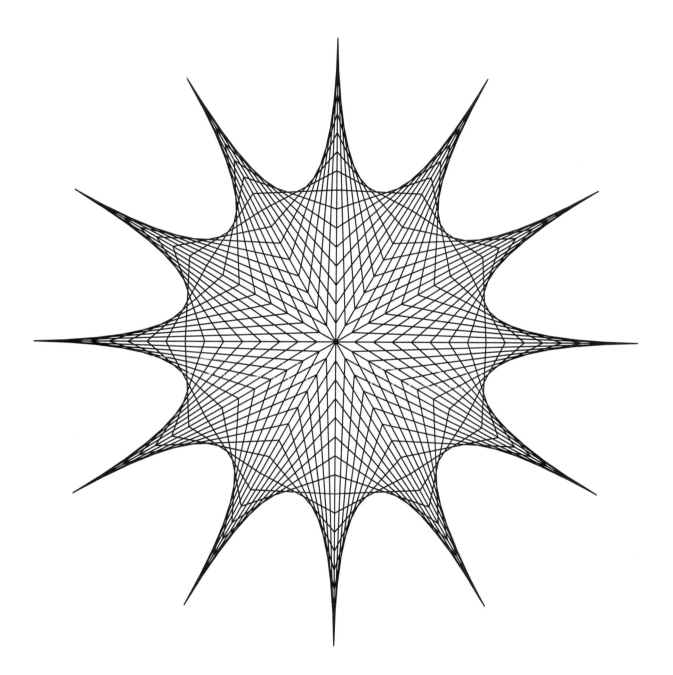

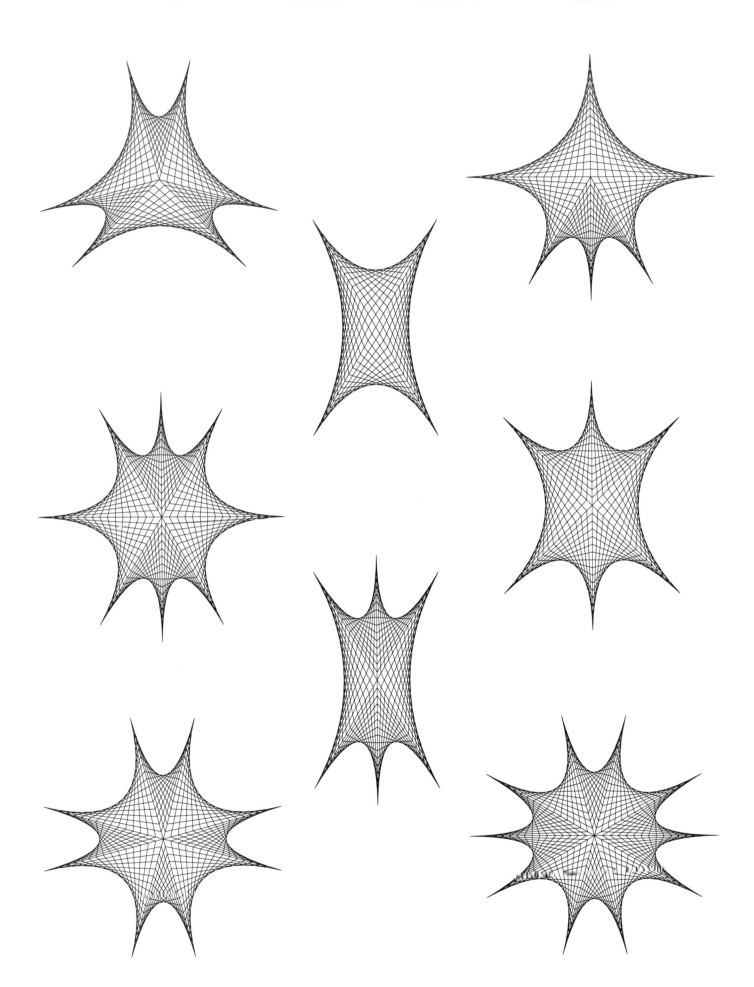

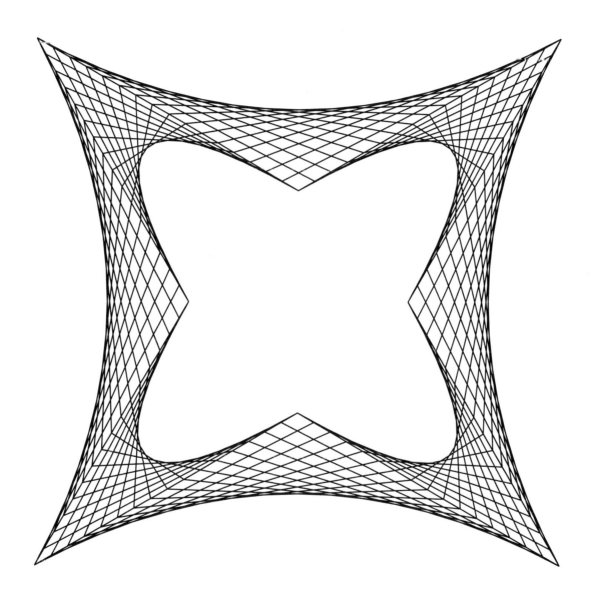

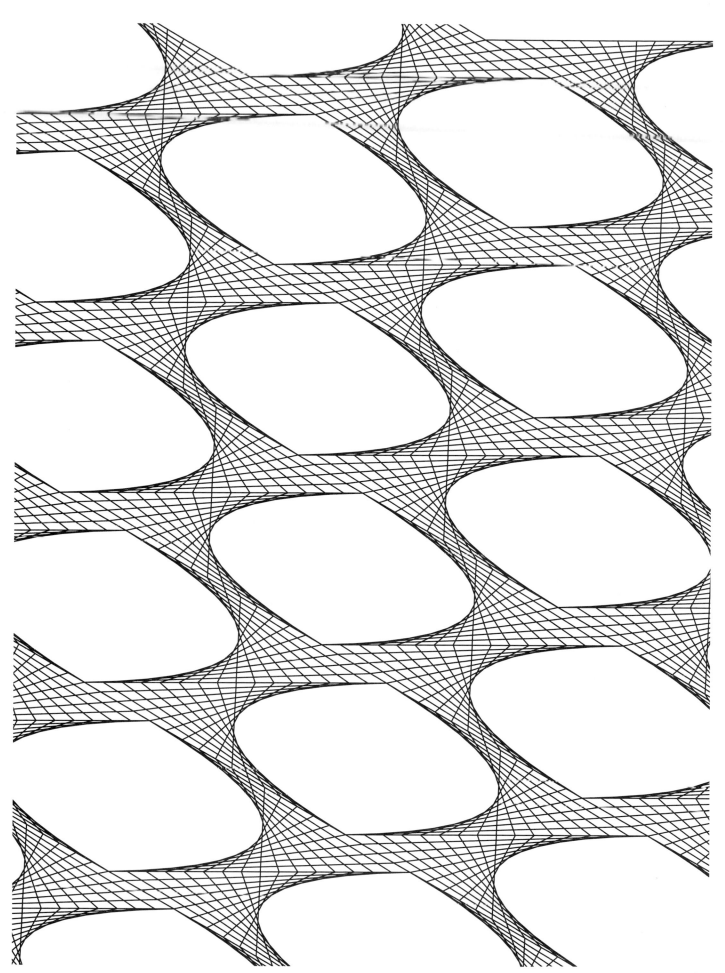

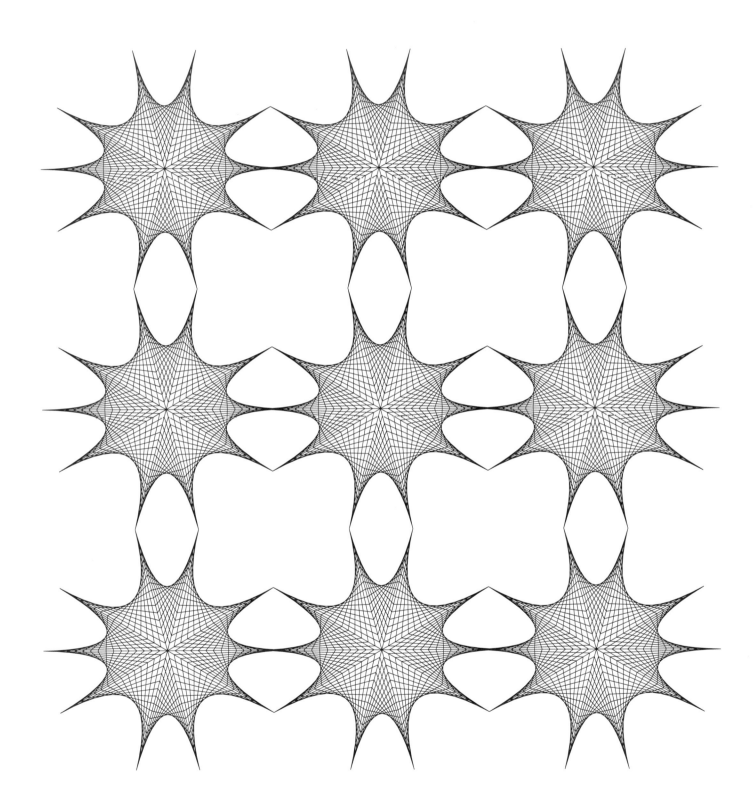

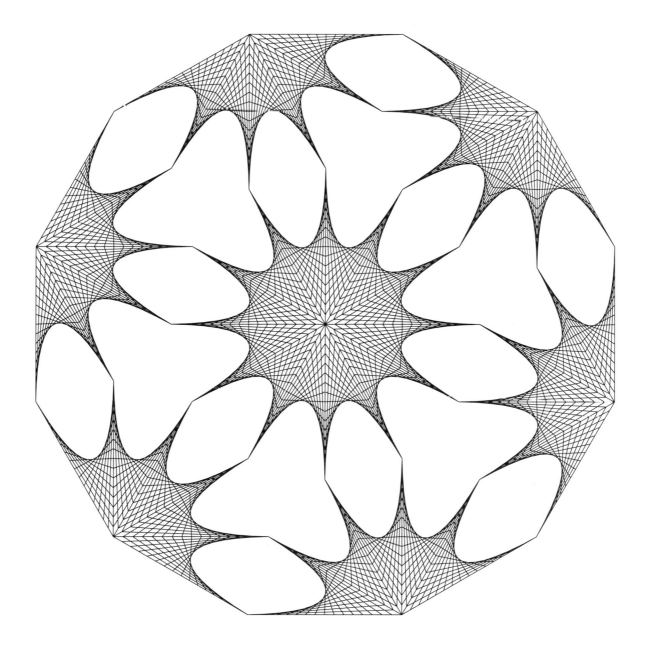

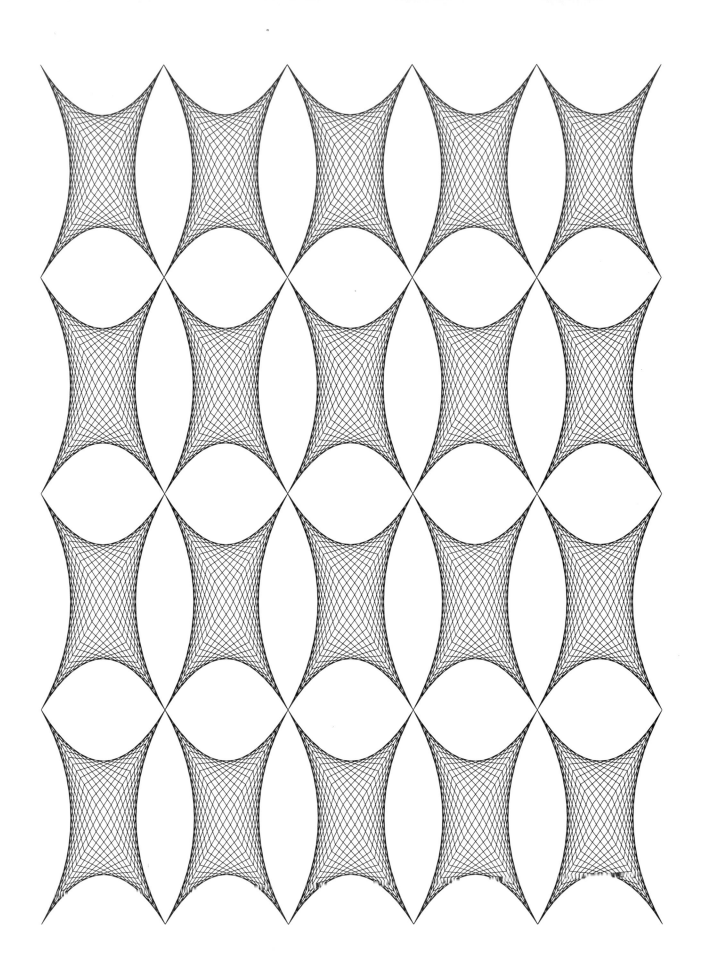

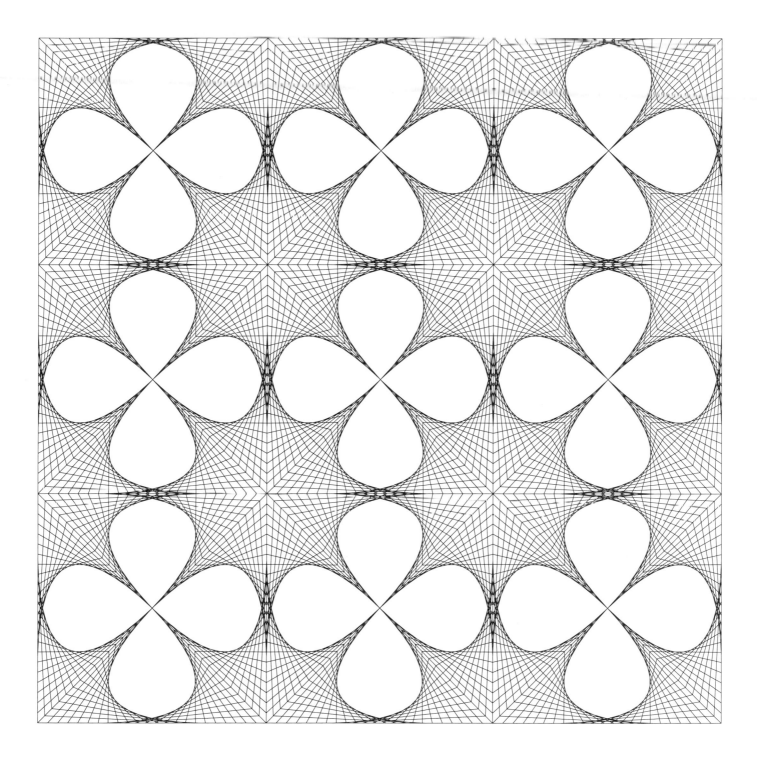

Line Designs Made from Composite of Two Shapes

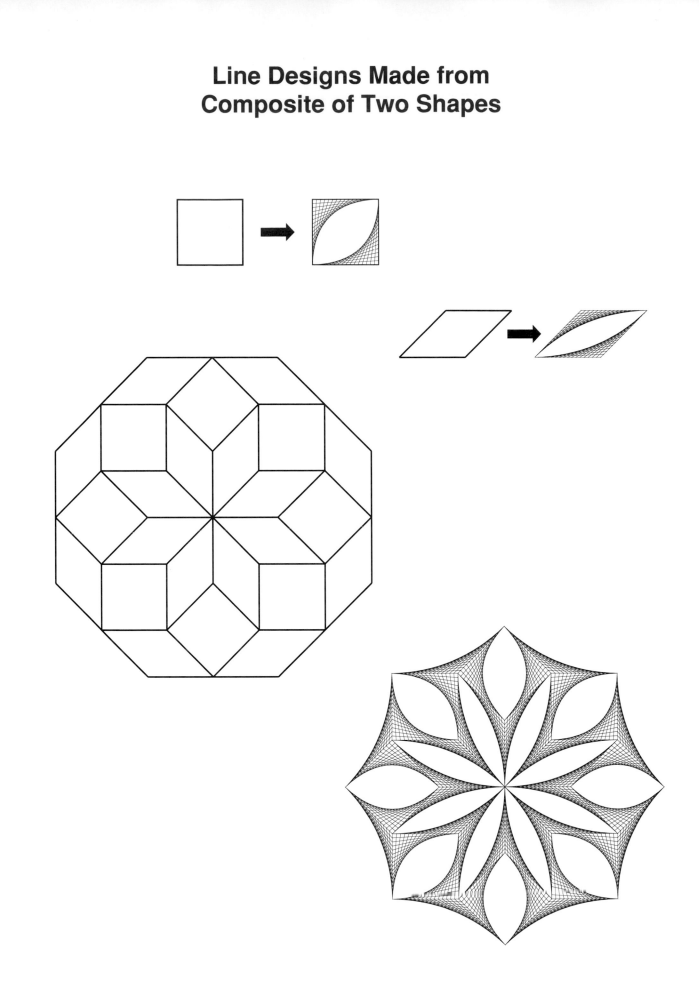

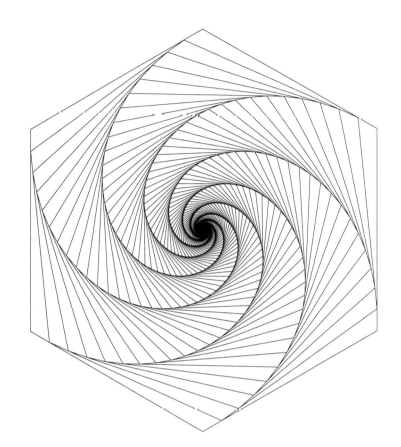

CHAPTER **5**

DESIGNS FROM
INSCRIBED POLYGONS

In addition to being formed within angles, line designs can be formed by inscribing successive polygons within each other. The term *inscribed polygon* means a polygon whose vertices all lie on a given closed geometric shape.

Two different approaches can be used to form the figures you see illustrated in this chapter. One approach is to form the smaller polygon within the larger by dividing the sides of the larger into equal numbers of equal segments. These division points are then connected by segments, much like we did with angle side divisions. A step-by-step explanation of the procedure is shown on the opposite page. This method can be very time consuming without the use of a computer drawing program, but it can be done.

In the examples on the right, each smaller triangle has its vertices established at the eighth of 10 divisions along the side of the larger triangle. Choice of the eighth division was purely arbitrary, but the nicest curves are established by chosing a point between 70% and 90% of the line length. Once the division point is chosen, that division ratio should remain constant throughout the design.

In the final design figure, the triangles disappear to a point and the straight sides of the triangles appear to form curves.

LINE DESIGNS

Step-by-Step Creation of a Line Design
of Triangles Inscribed Within Triangles
(Method 1)

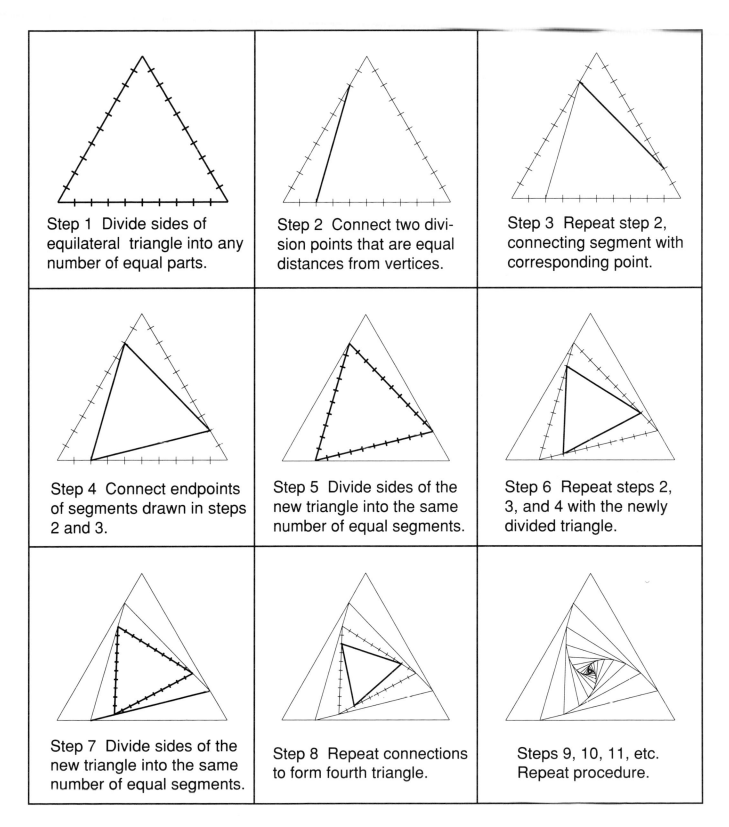

Step 1 Divide sides of equilateral triangle into any number of equal parts.

Step 2 Connect two division points that are equal distances from vertices.

Step 3 Repeat step 2, connecting segment with corresponding point.

Step 4 Connect endpoints of segments drawn in steps 2 and 3.

Step 5 Divide sides of the new triangle into the same number of equal segments.

Step 6 Repeat steps 2, 3, and 4 with the newly divided triangle.

Step 7 Divide sides of the new triangle into the same number of equal segments.

Step 8 Repeat connections to form fourth triangle.

Steps 9, 10, 11, etc. Repeat procedure.

Designs developed by inscribing regular polygons within similar regular polygons could be described as a series of two-step transformations. First, the polygon is reduced to a smaller, similar triangle; then it is rotated about its centroid until the vertices lie on the larger shape. These two steps are then repeated as long as the designer chooses.

Since the larger and smaller regular polygons have the same centroid, all vertices of each polygon lie the same distance from the rotation point. It is for this reason that the smaller polygon, when rotated into position on the larger polygon, will have all vertices lie on the larger.

The second method for creating these types of designs is shown on the opposite page. First, the larger triangle is reduced by some arbitrary percentage. (70% –90% is considered to give the most pleasing curve illusions.) Secondly, the reduced triangle is rotated about its centroid to a position where all vertices of the smaller triangle lie on the larger triangle.

Pages 82 and 83 show two methods of creating designs where squares are inscribed in squares. Both techniques, in general, are the same as those described with triangles.

The remainder of this chapter shows designs created from various regular polygons and combinations of these designs.

Step-by-Step Creation of a Line Design
of Triangles Inscribed Within Triangles
(Method 2)

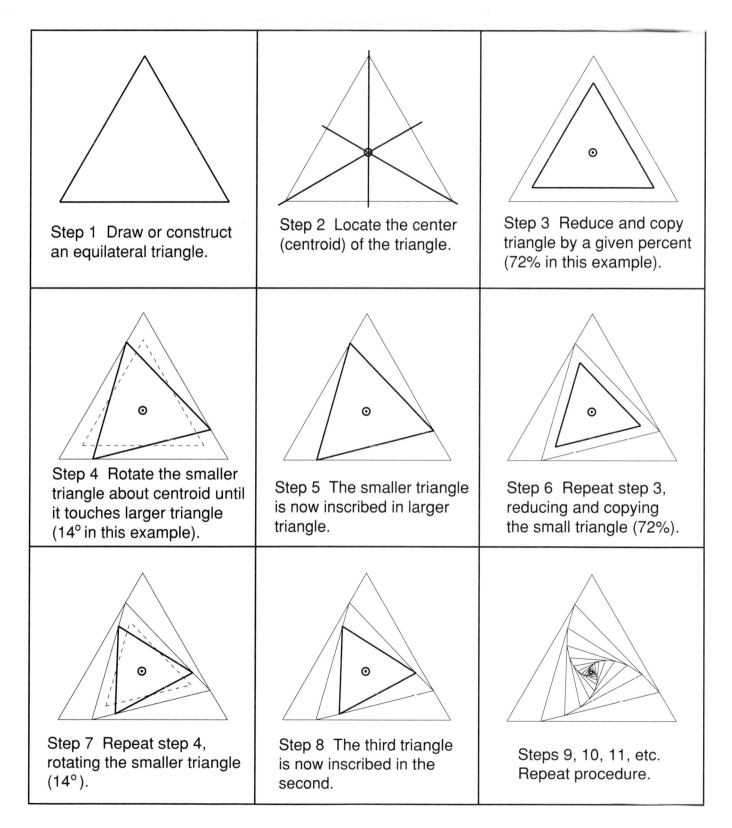

Step 1 Draw or construct an equilateral triangle.

Step 2 Locate the center (centroid) of the triangle.

Step 3 Reduce and copy triangle by a given percent (72% in this example).

Step 4 Rotate the smaller triangle about centroid until it touches larger triangle (14° in this example).

Step 5 The smaller triangle is now inscribed in larger triangle.

Step 6 Repeat step 3, reducing and copying the small triangle (72%).

Step 7 Repeat step 4, rotating the smaller triangle (14°).

Step 8 The third triangle is now inscribed in the second.

Steps 9, 10, 11, etc. Repeat procedure.

Step-by-Step Creation of a Line Design
of Squares Inscribed Within Squares
(Method 1)

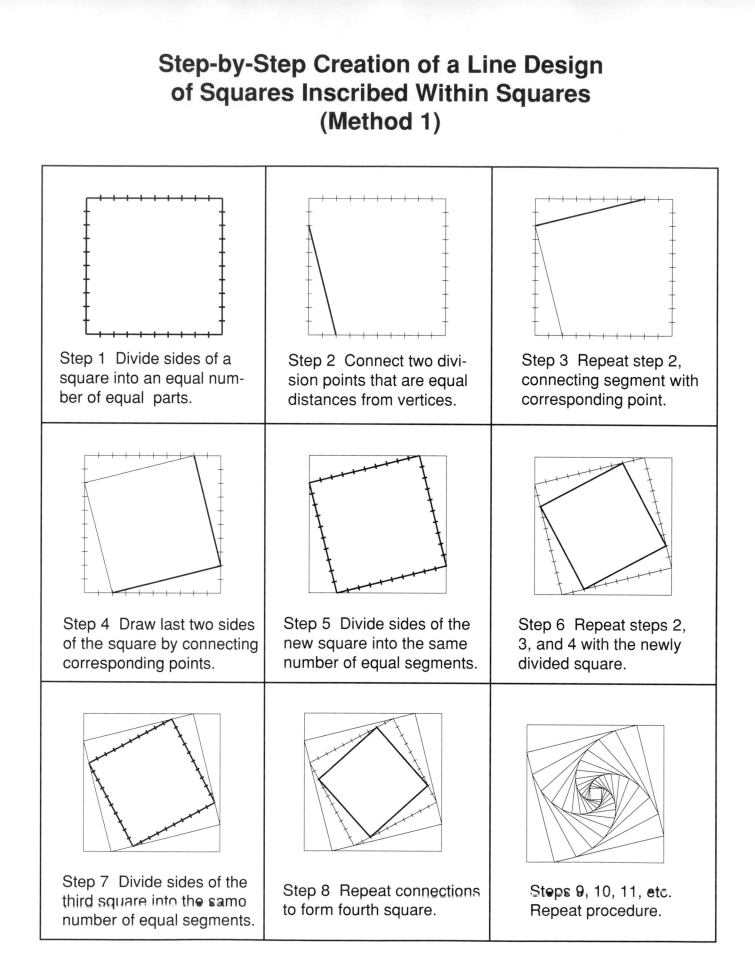

Step 1 Divide sides of a square into an equal number of equal parts.

Step 2 Connect two division points that are equal distances from vertices.

Step 3 Repeat step 2, connecting segment with corresponding point.

Step 4 Draw last two sides of the square by connecting corresponding points.

Step 5 Divide sides of the new square into the same number of equal segments.

Step 6 Repeat steps 2, 3, and 4 with the newly divided square.

Step 7 Divide sides of the third square into the same number of equal segments.

Step 8 Repeat connections to form fourth square.

Steps 9, 10, 11, etc. Repeat procedure.

Step-by-Step Creation of a Line Design
of Squares Inscribed Within Squares
(Method 2)

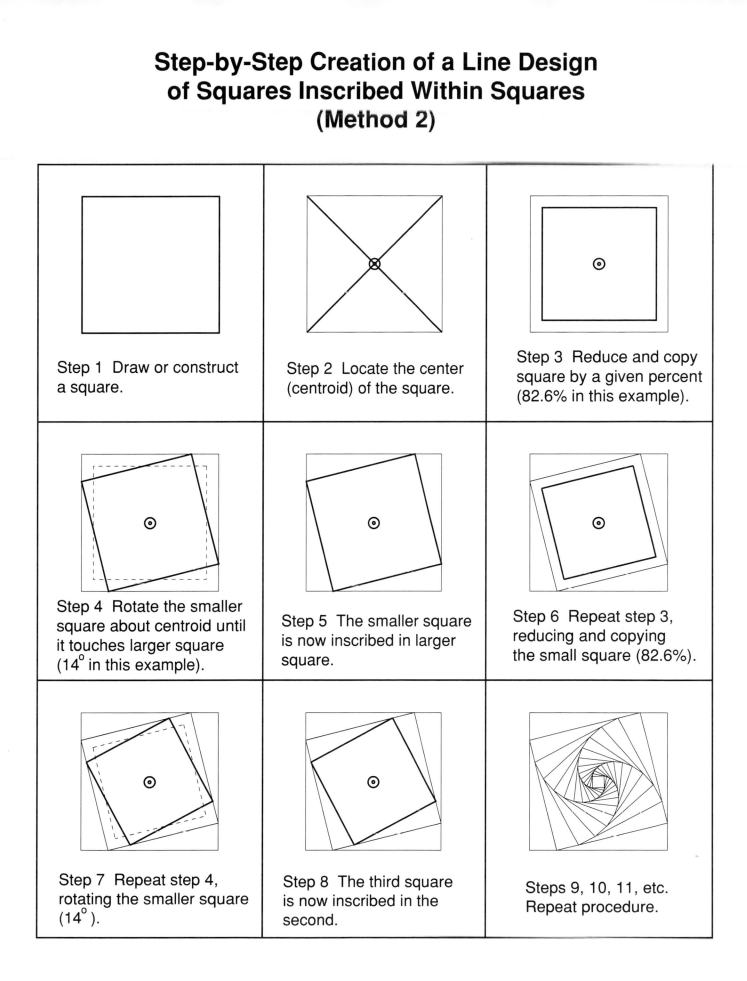

Step 1 Draw or construct a square.

Step 2 Locate the center (centroid) of the square.

Step 3 Reduce and copy square by a given percent (82.6% in this example).

Step 4 Rotate the smaller square about centroid until it touches larger square (14° in this example).

Step 5 The smaller square is now inscribed in larger square.

Step 6 Repeat step 3, reducing and copying the small square (82.6%).

Step 7 Repeat step 4, rotating the smaller square (14°).

Step 8 The third square is now inscribed in the second.

Steps 9, 10, 11, etc. Repeat procedure.

When making a line design by inscribing a regular polygon within a regular polygon, the reduced polygons can be rotated either in a clockwise or counterclockwise direction. Figures 5-1 and 5-2, below, show the two options.

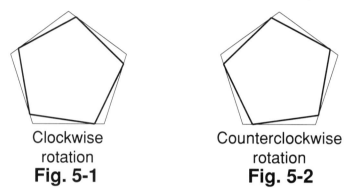

Clockwise
rotation
Fig. 5-1

Counterclockwise
rotation
Fig. 5-2

The final result of the clockwise and counterclockwise designs are shown below in Figures 5-3 and 5-4. Notice that one design is the mirror reflection of the other.

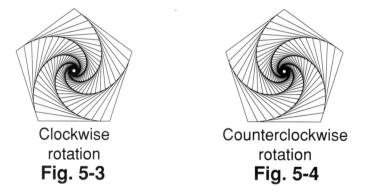

Clockwise
rotation
Fig. 5-3

Counterclockwise
rotation
Fig. 5-4

If the reduction of the polygon is too great, the reduced shape will not inscribe in the original shape. Notice in the chart on the opposite page that the greater the number of sides the more limited the reduction of the figure.

Chart for Determining Reductions And Rotations for Inscribed Polygons

Rotation in Degrees

Percent Reduction	Equilateral Triangle	Square	Regular Pentagon	Regular Hexagon	Regular Octagon
96%	1.5	2.4	3.5	4.4	6.7
94%	2.1	3.8	5.3	7.1	11.7
92%	2.9	5.2	7.6	10.3	-----
90%	3.8	6.8	10.0	14.2	-----
88%	4.6	8.4	12.8	19.8	-----
86%	5.5	10.3	16.1	-----	-----
84%	6.5	12.3	20.3	-----	-----
82%	7.5	14.6	26.4	-----	-----
80%	8.7	17.1	-----	-----	-----
78%	9.8	20.0	-----	-----	-----
76%	11.1	23.3	-----	-----	-----
74%	12.5	27.6	-----	-----	-----
72%	13.9	34.0	-----	-----	-----
70%	15.6	-----	-----	-----	-----
68%	17.2	-----	-----	-----	-----
66%	19.4	-----	-----	-----	-----

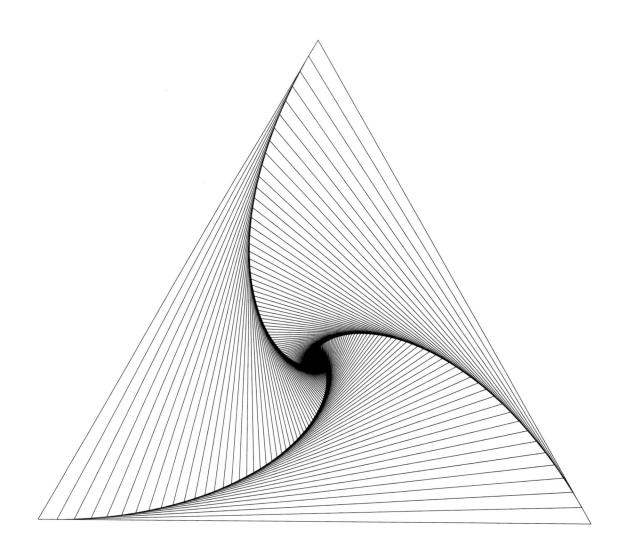

Various Reductions
and Rotations of
Inscribed Triangles

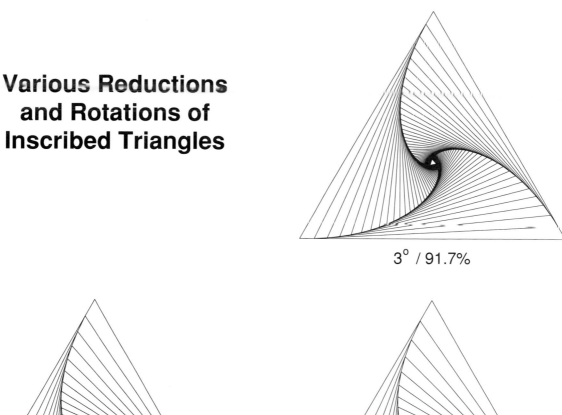

3° / 91.7%

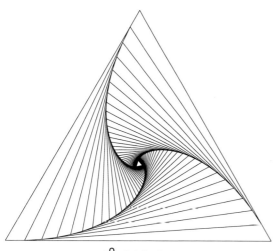

4° / 89.4%

5° / 87 %

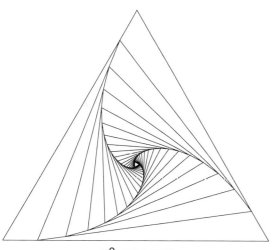

8° / 81.2%

10° / 77.9%

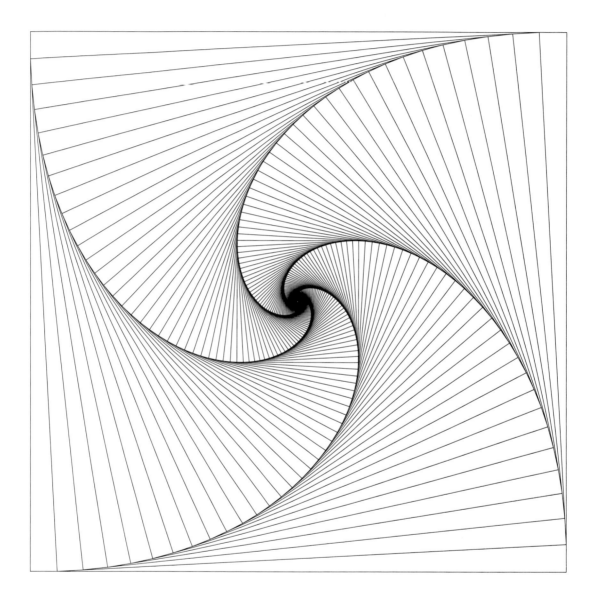

Various Reductions and Rotations of Inscribed Squares

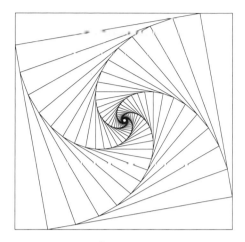

10° / 86.3%

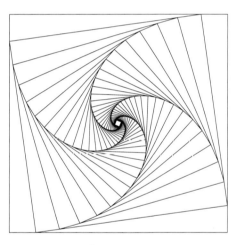

8° / 88.5%

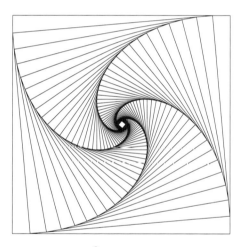

6° / 92.2%

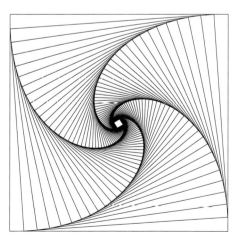

4° / 93.6%

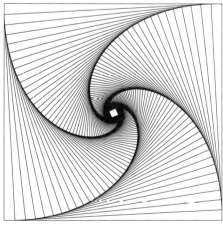

3° / 95.1%

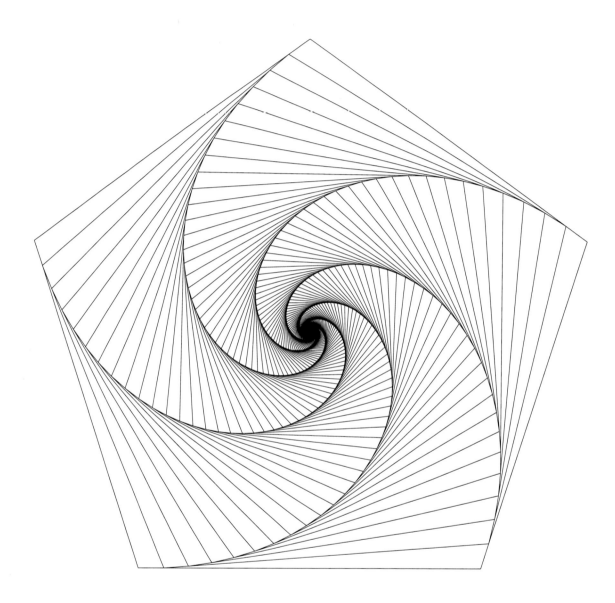

Various Reductions and Rotations of Inscribed Squares

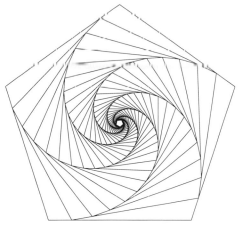

10° / 90%

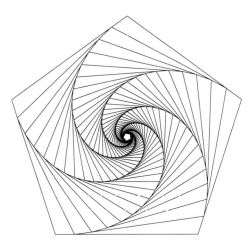

8° / 91.7%

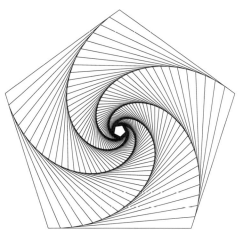

5° / 94.4%

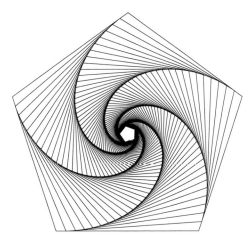

4° / 95.5%

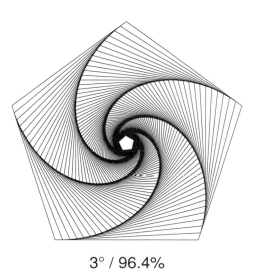

3° / 96.4%

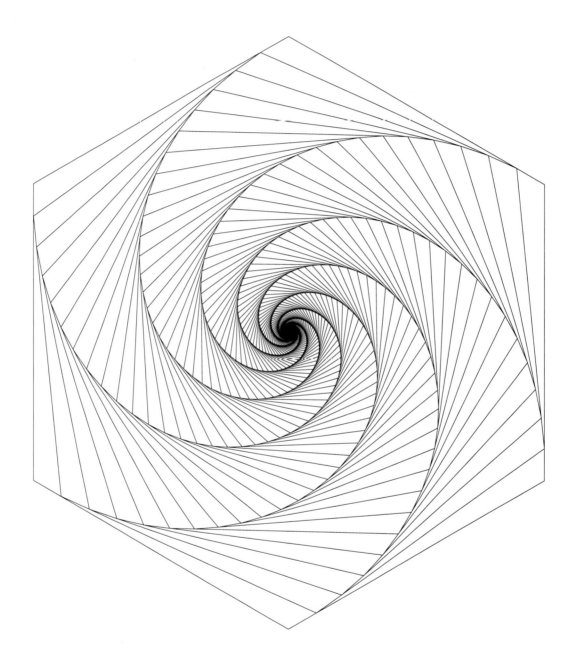

Various Reductions
and Rotations of
Inscribed Squares

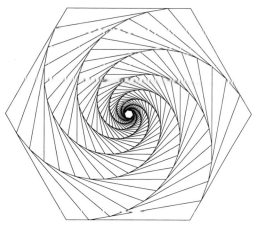

10° / 92.2%

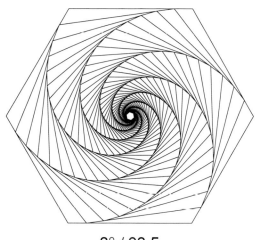

8° / 93.5

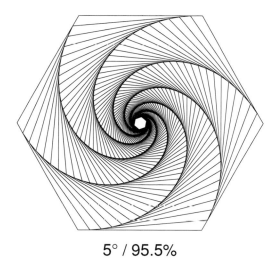

5° / 95.5%

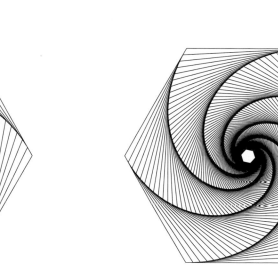

4° / 96.4%

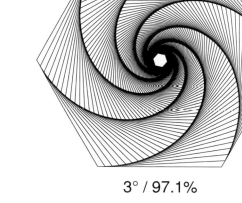

3° / 97.1%

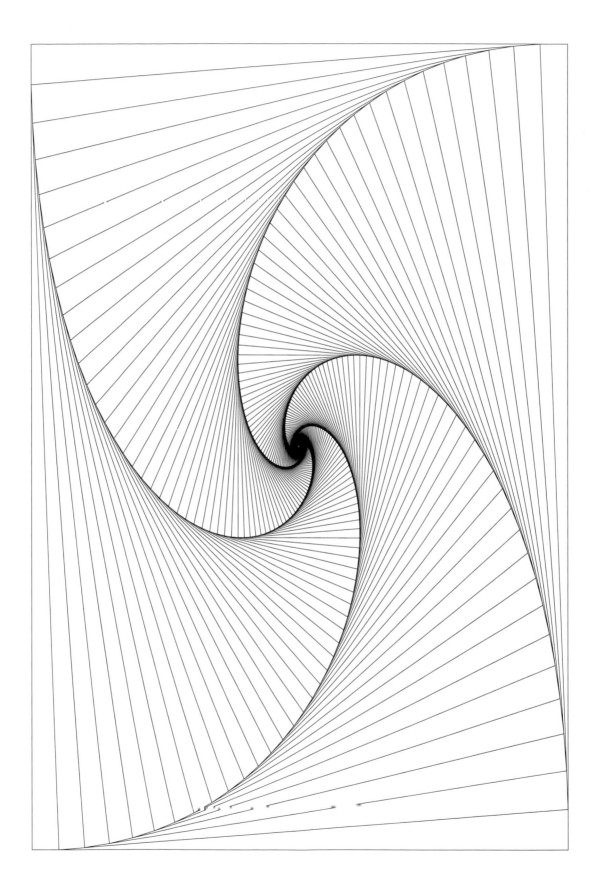

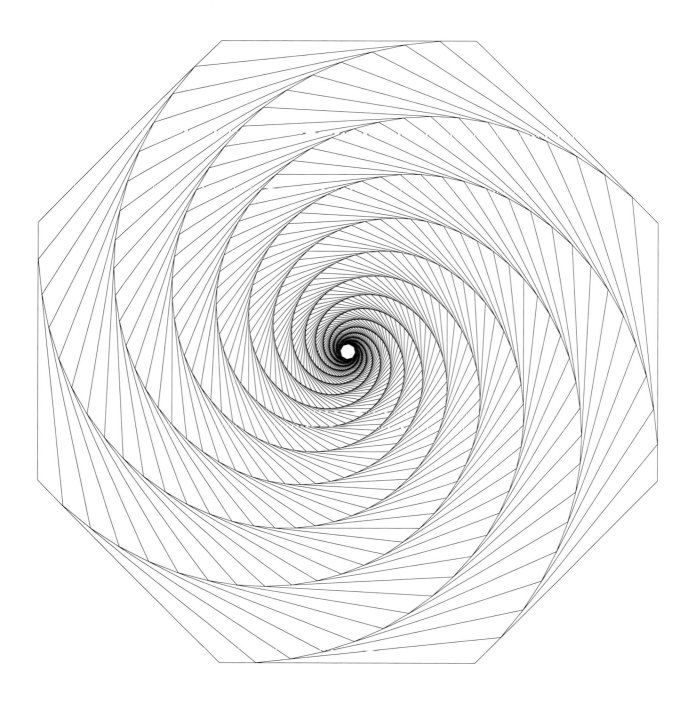

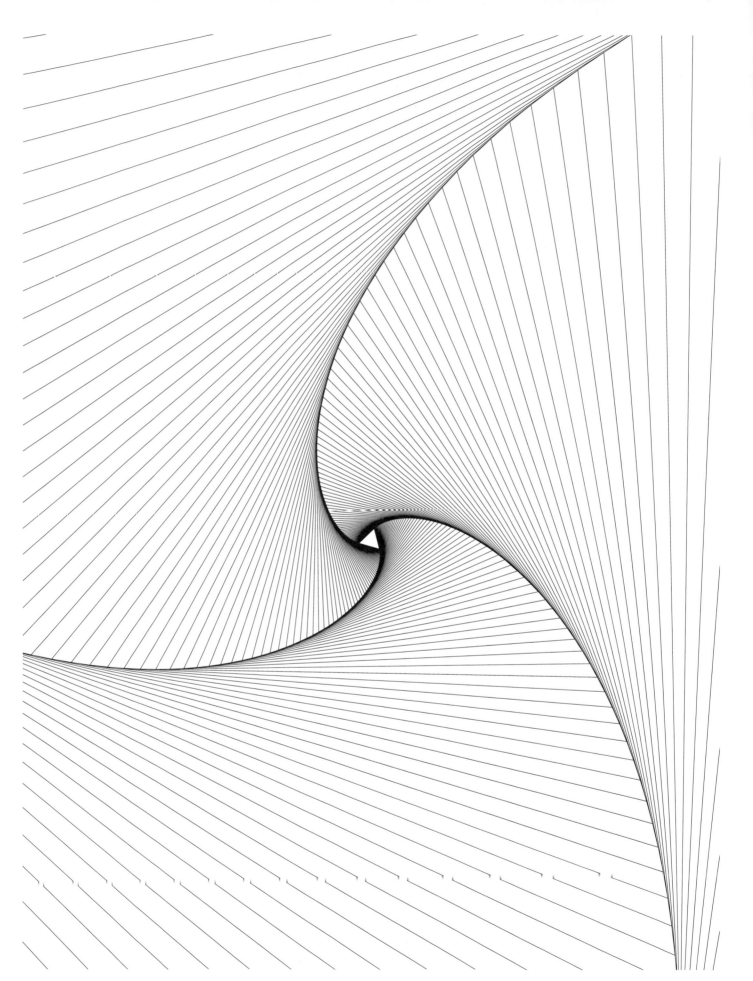

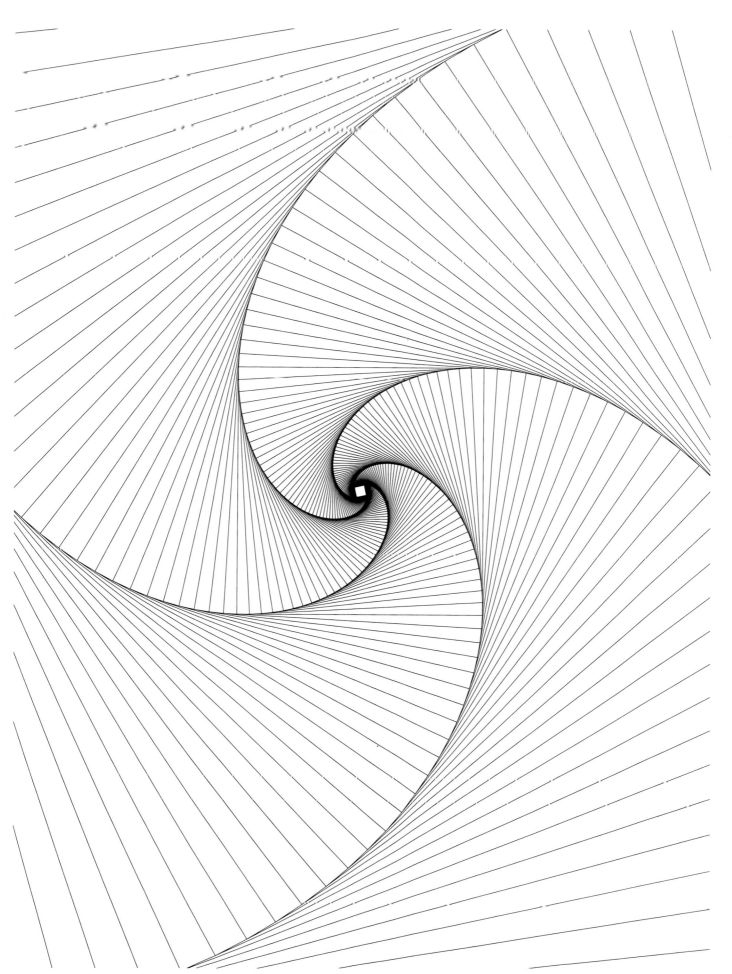

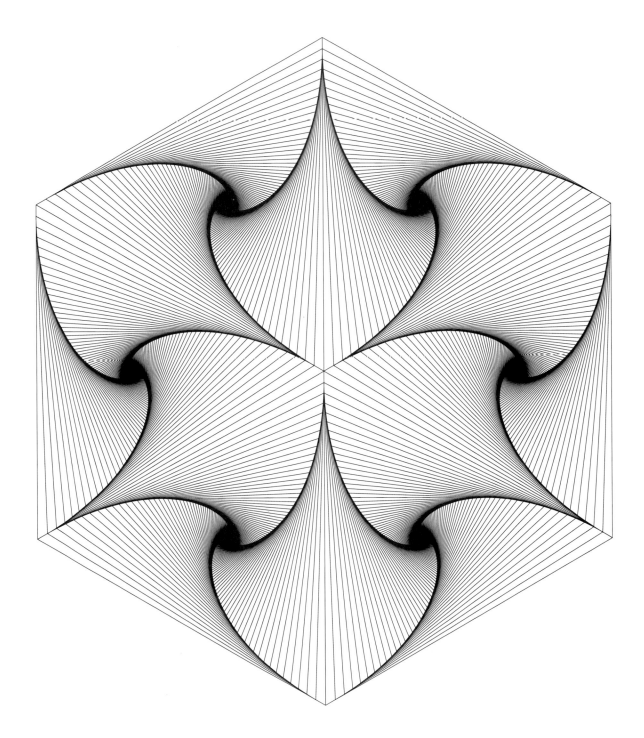

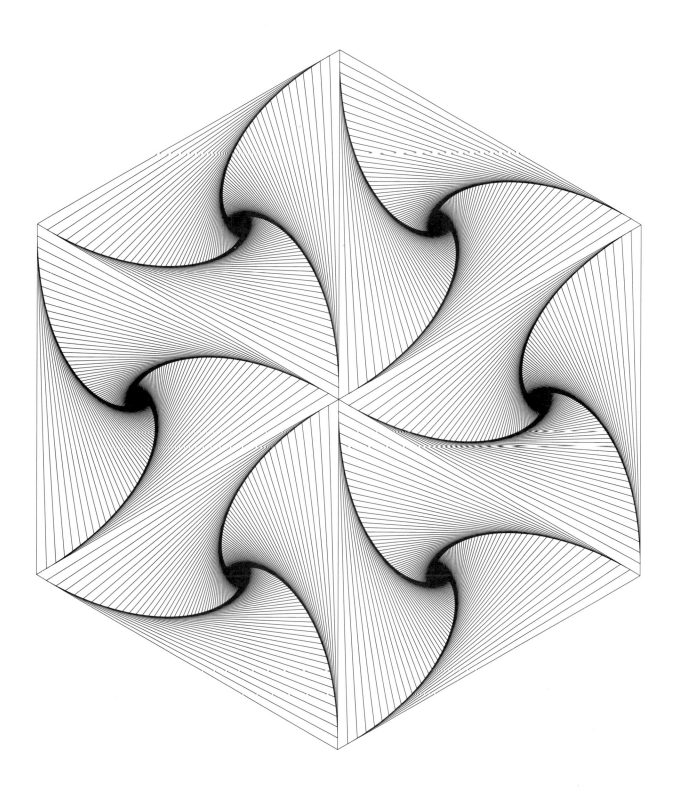

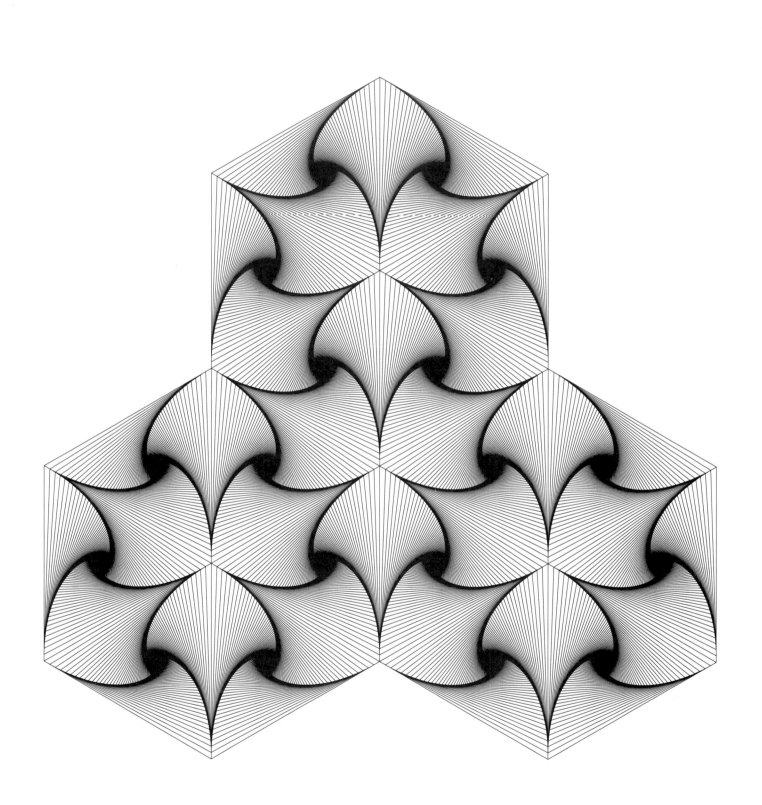

102 Introduction to Line Designs

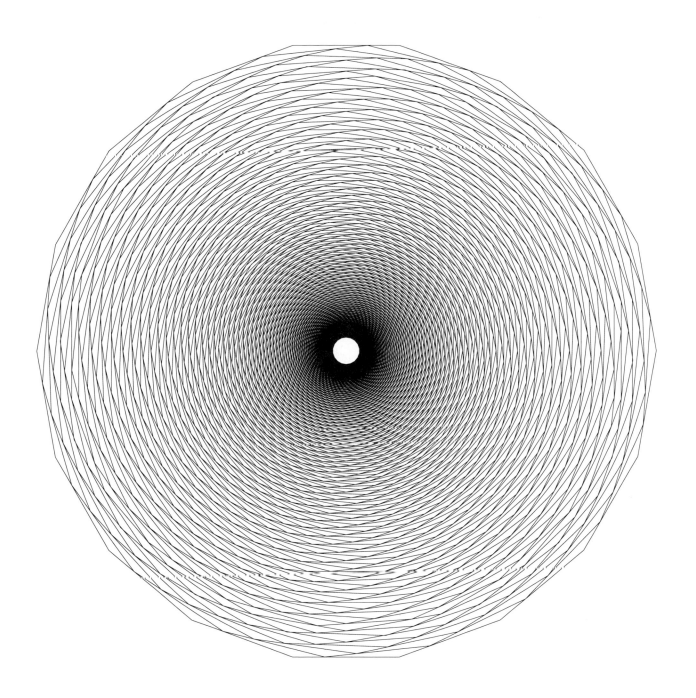

Introduction to Line Designs

Step-by-Step Creation of a Line Design of Pentagons Inscribed Within Pentagons Where Rotations Alternate Directions

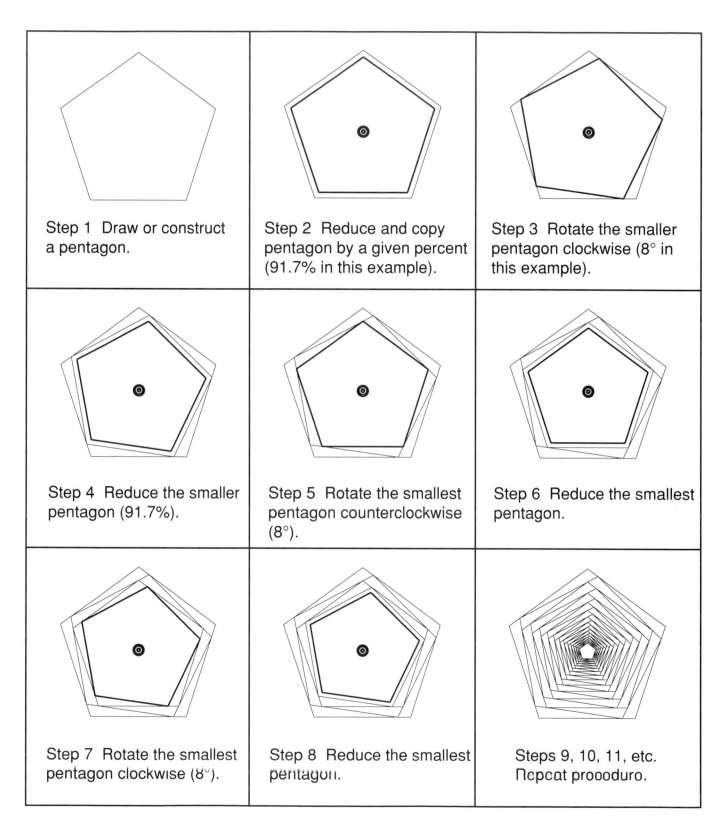

Step 1 Draw or construct a pentagon.

Step 2 Reduce and copy pentagon by a given percent (91.7% in this example).

Step 3 Rotate the smaller pentagon clockwise (8° in this example).

Step 4 Reduce the smaller pentagon (91.7%).

Step 5 Rotate the smallest pentagon counterclockwise (8°).

Step 6 Reduce the smallest pentagon.

Step 7 Rotate the smallest pentagon clockwise (8°).

Step 8 Reduce the smallest pentagon.

Steps 9, 10, 11, etc. Repeat procedure.

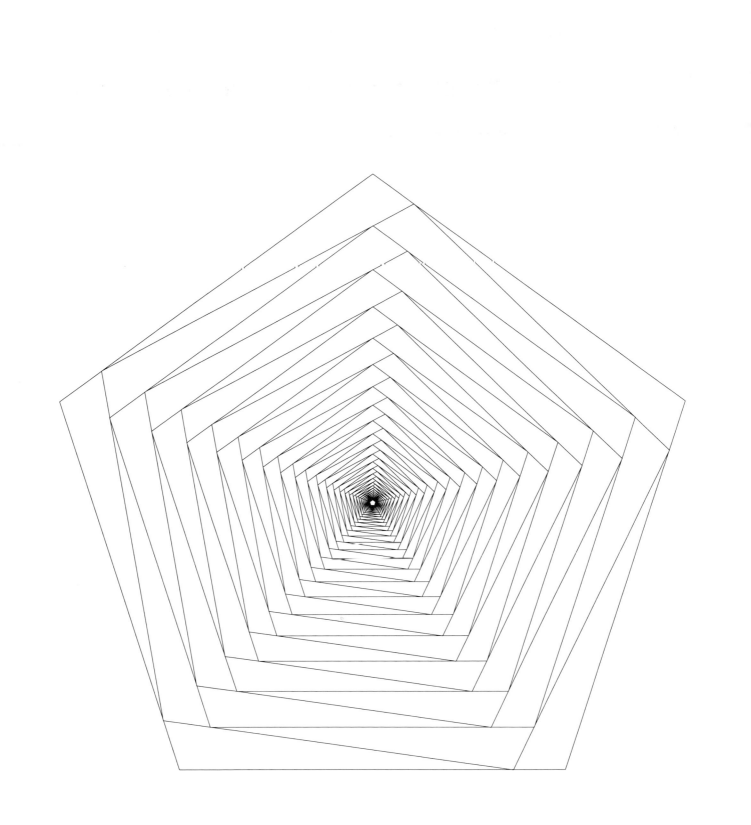

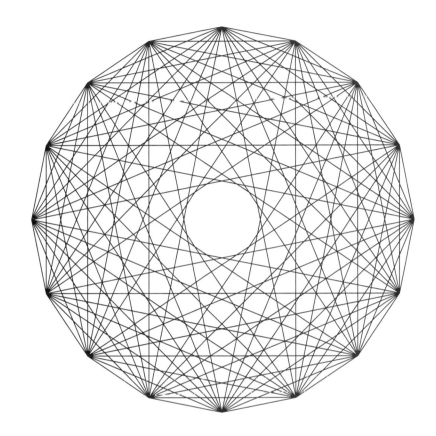

CHAPTER **6**
DESIGNS FROM
DIAGONALS AND CHORDS

A diagonal of a polygon is a line segment joining any two nonadjacent vertices. If all the diagonals are drawn in regular polygons containing 12 or more sides, illusions of circles exist. We can think of these as line designs since straight lines appear to be forming curves.

The four figures on the opposite page show all the diagonals in 8-, 12-, 16-, and 24-sided regular polygons. Notice the illusion of circles being formed. The greater the number of vertices, the more the figures appear to form circles. The 24-sided polygon in Fig. 6-8 almost appears to be a circle itself.

Chords of a circle, arc, or ellipse are line segments joining any two points on one of those figures. If chords of a circle are equally spaced, their intersections will give the same illusion of concentric circles.

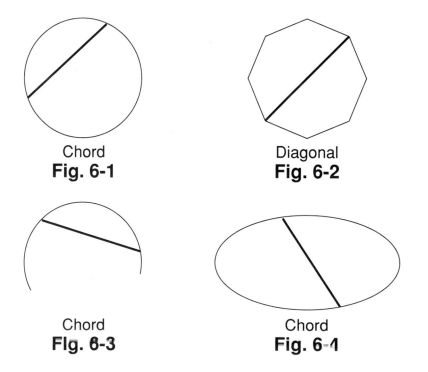

Chord
Fig. 6-1

Diagonal
Fig. 6-2

Chord
Fig. 6-3

Chord
Fig. 6-4

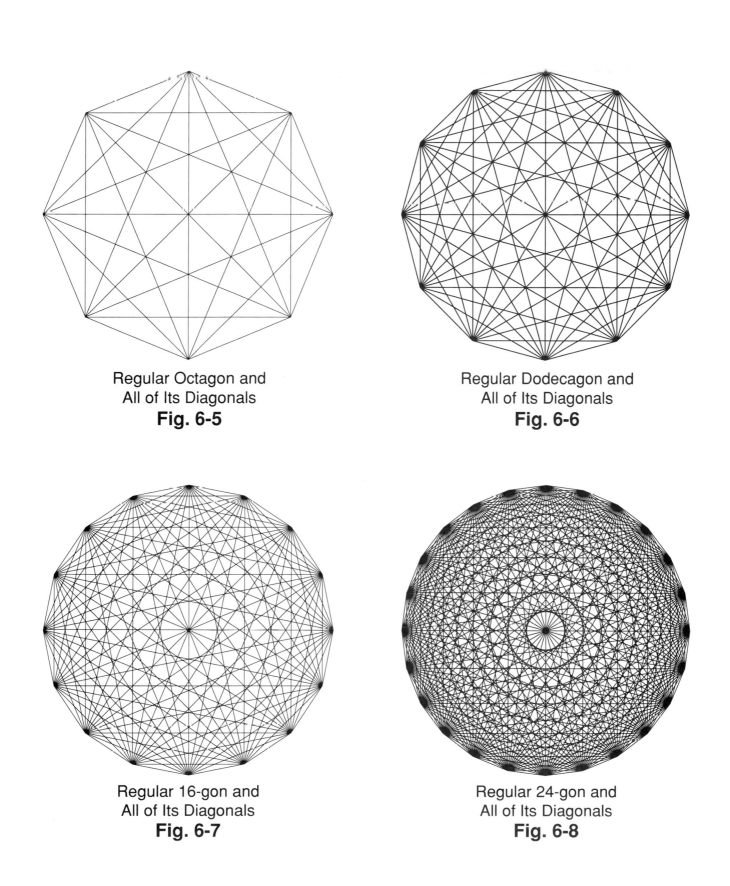

Regular Octagon and
All of Its Diagonals
Fig. 6-5

Regular Dodecagon and
All of Its Diagonals
Fig. 6-6

Regular 16-gon and
All of Its Diagonals
Fig. 6-7

Regular 24-gon and
All of Its Diagonals
Fig. 6-8

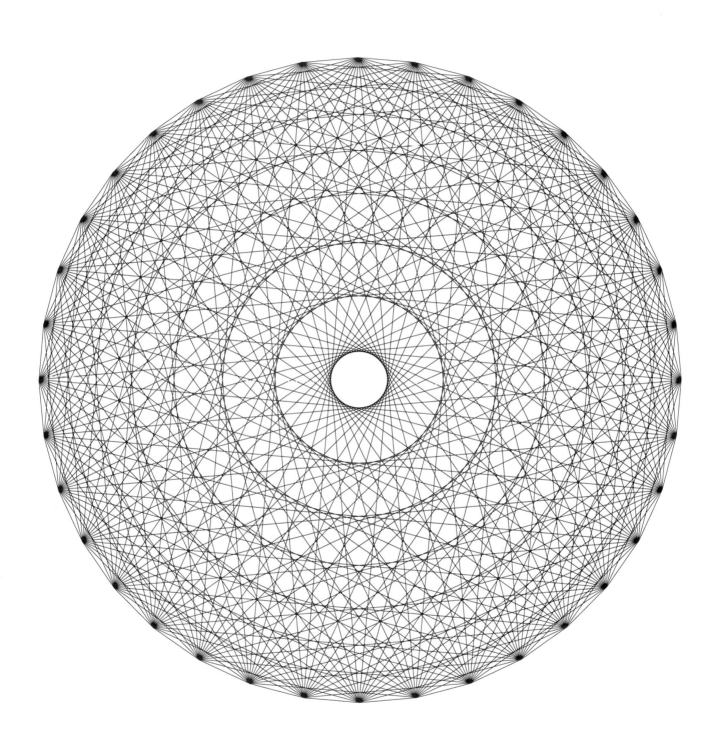

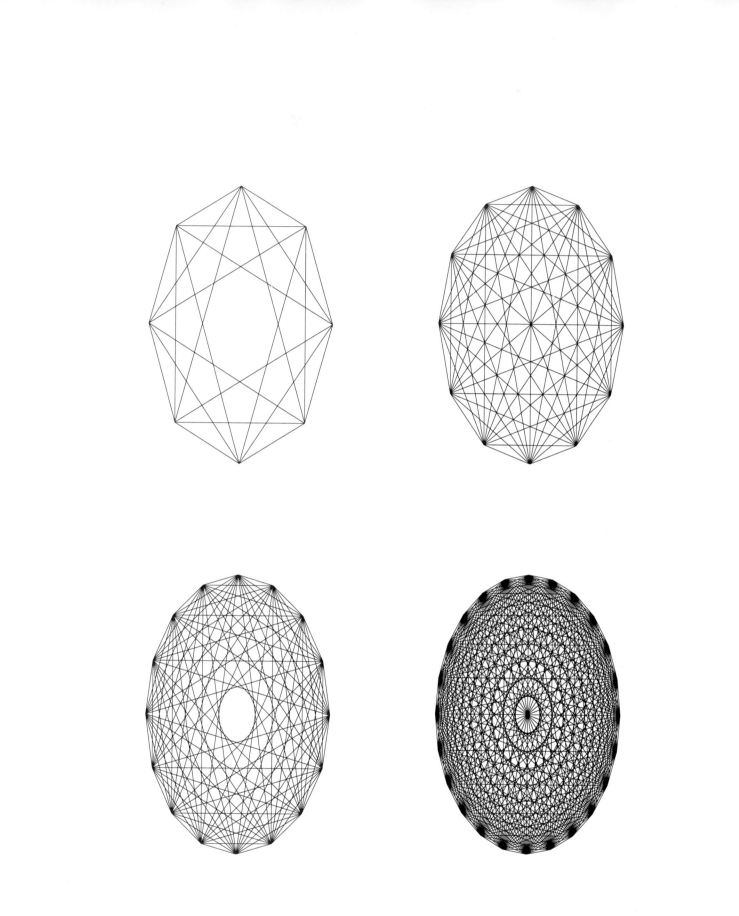

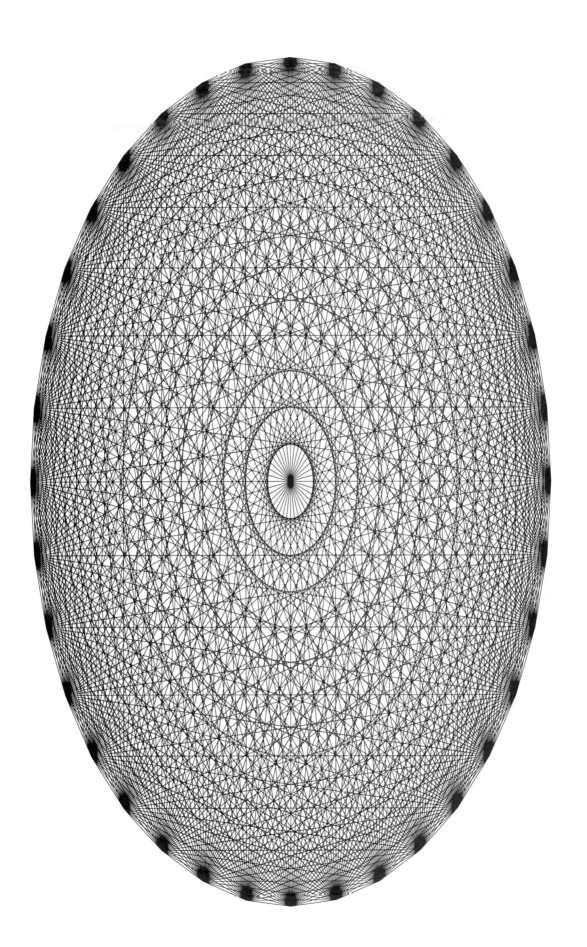

The designs on the opposite page are made from chords of a circle that has been divided into 36 equal parts. Fig. 6-9 shows the connection of every third division point. Fig. 6-10 shows every third, fifth, and seventh point connected. The other figures continue in the same pattern.

Circle illusions come from the fact that equal chords of the same circle lie equal distances from the center of the circle. Using this technique, a variety of designs creating the illusion of circles can be drawn.

LINE DESIGNS

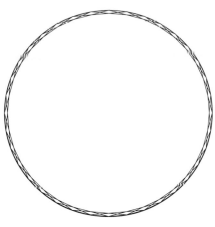

Fig. 6-9

Fig. 6-10

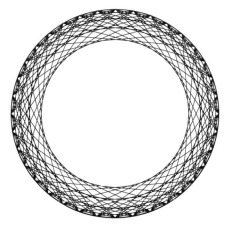

Fig. 6-11

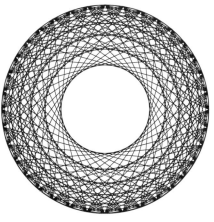

Fig. 6-12

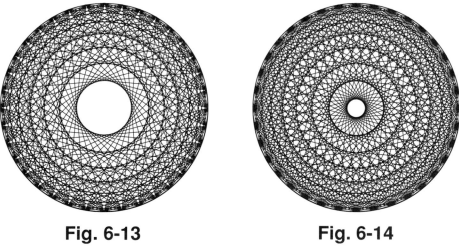

Fig. 6-13

Fig. 6-14

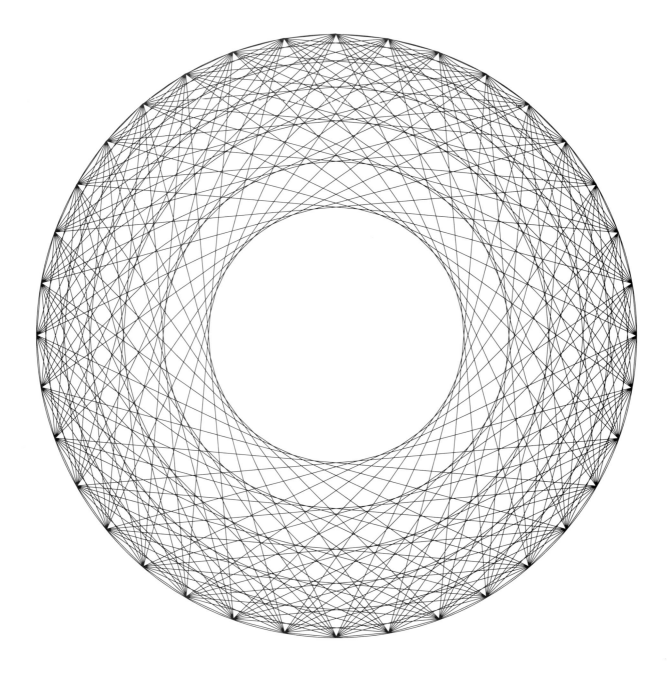

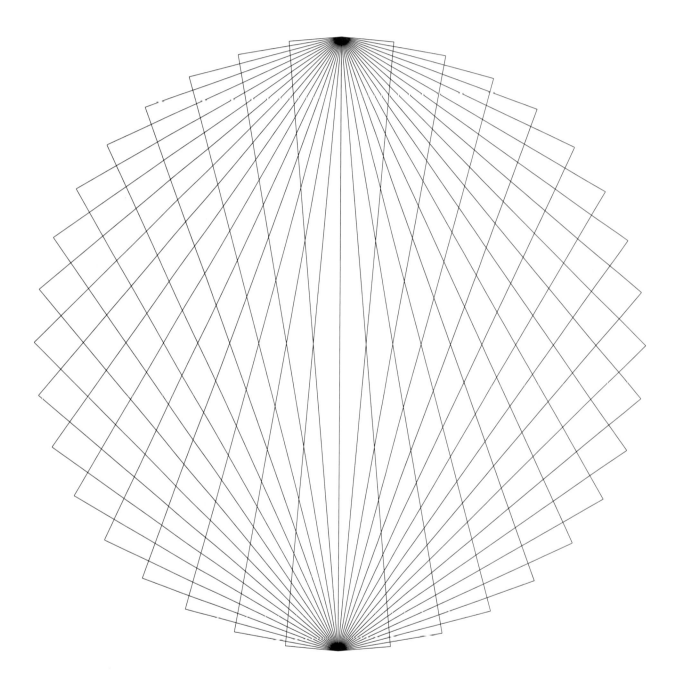

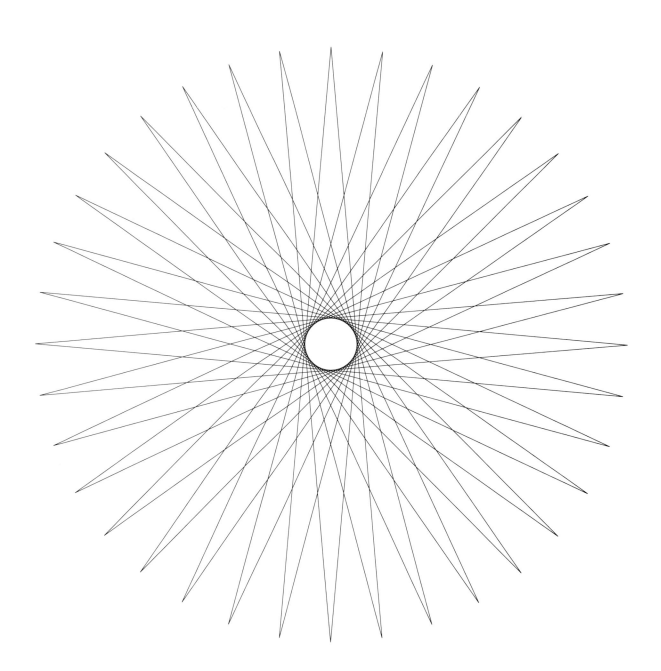

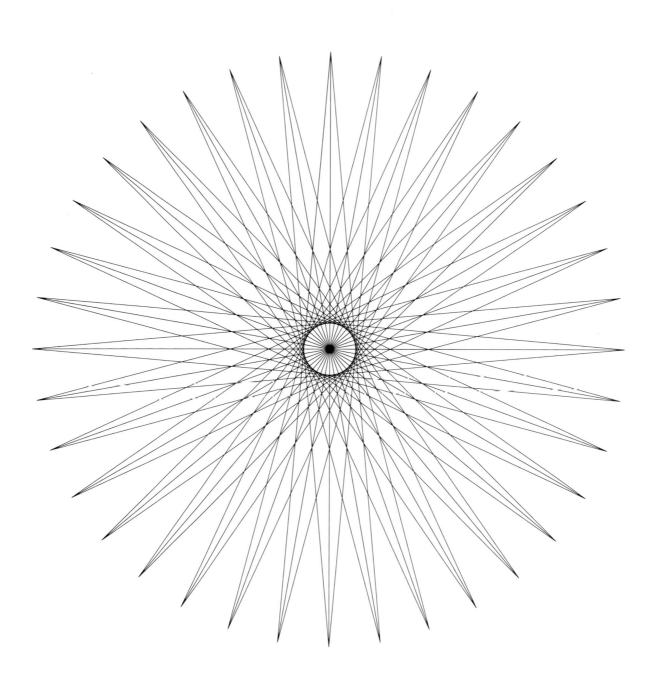

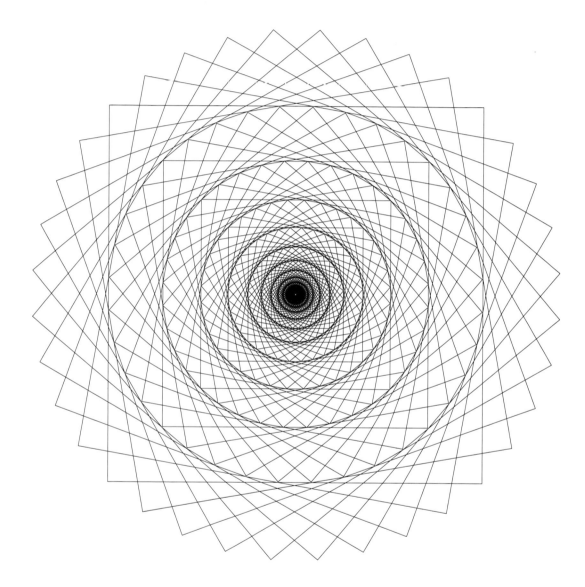

CHAPTER **7**

OVERLAPPING
DESIGNS

123

When line designs are created in more than one angle within a polygon or group of polygons, lines often overlap. Overlapping designs in this chapter can be classified into two types: (1) transparent and (2) opaque. Examples of transparent designs are shown on the pages in the first half of this chapter; opaque designs are shown in the latter half.

Opaque designs block out the overlapping portion of the design. Opaquing lines may be done on pencil and ink drawings by first drawing all the lines in pencil, then erasing the "back lines," and, finally, inking in the lines that you want to remain. With a computer, the "back lines" can be blocked out by created a solid white shape the exact shape of the overlap. The front design prints over the white shape, while the opaque, white shape covers the "back lines." This procedure with the computer is usually available only on the more sophisticated software drawing programs.

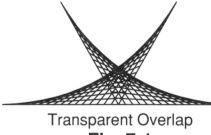

Transparent Overlap
Fig. 7-1

Opaque Overlap
Fig. 7-2

To accomplish an opaque effect with thread or string art, you would first need to create a pencil drawing and select various points where the thread or string would need to go behind the surface on which you are working.

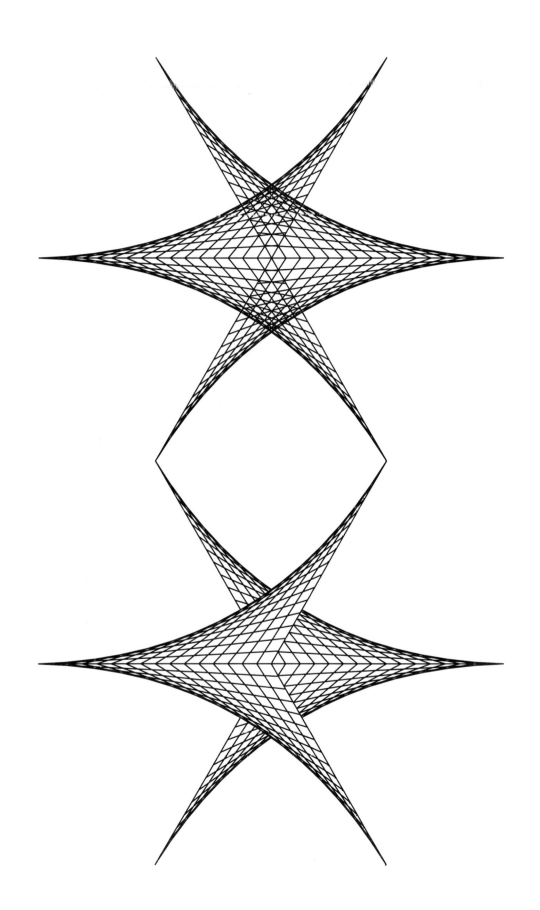

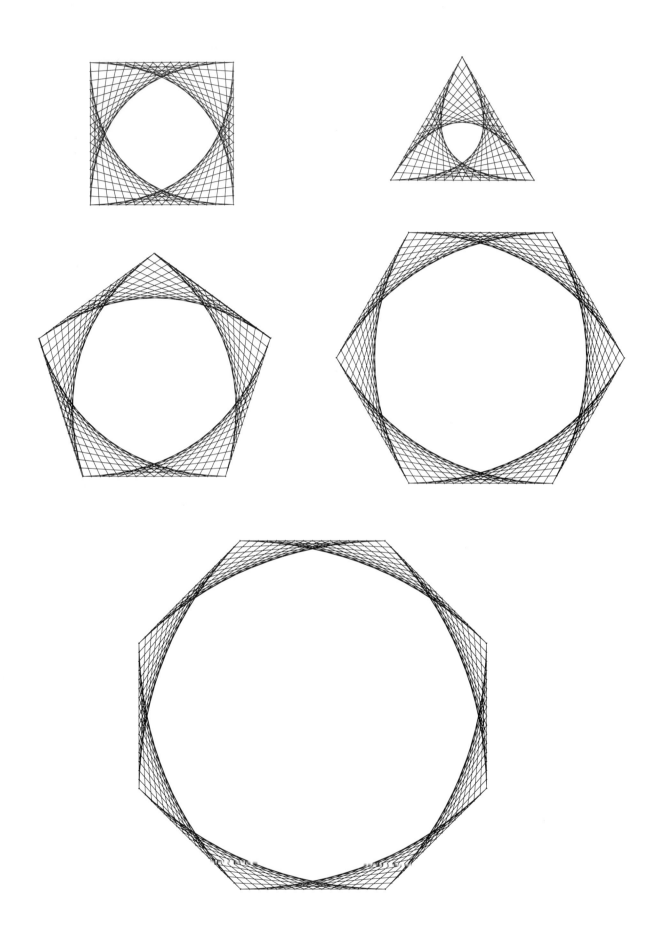

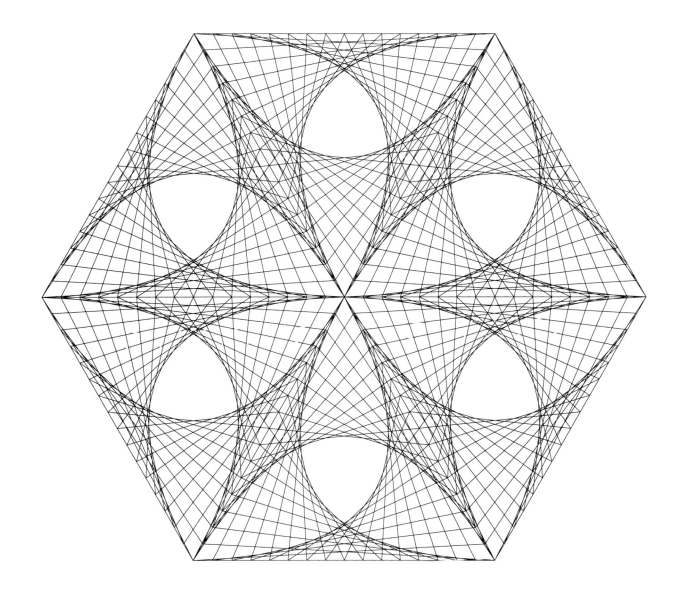

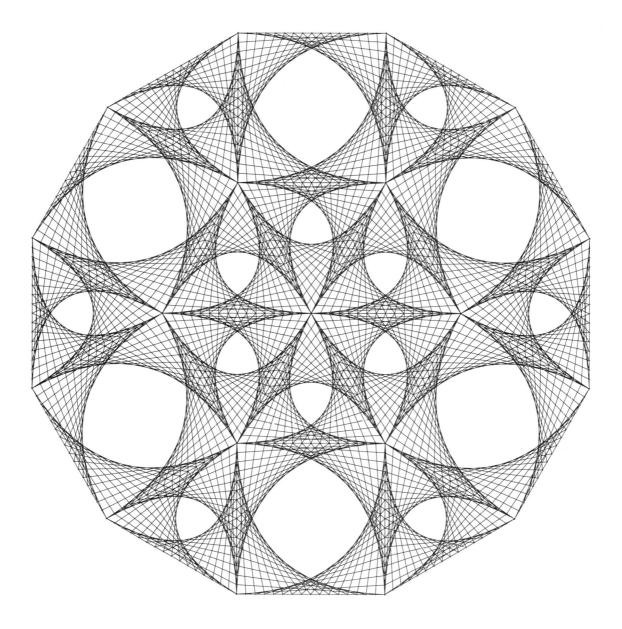

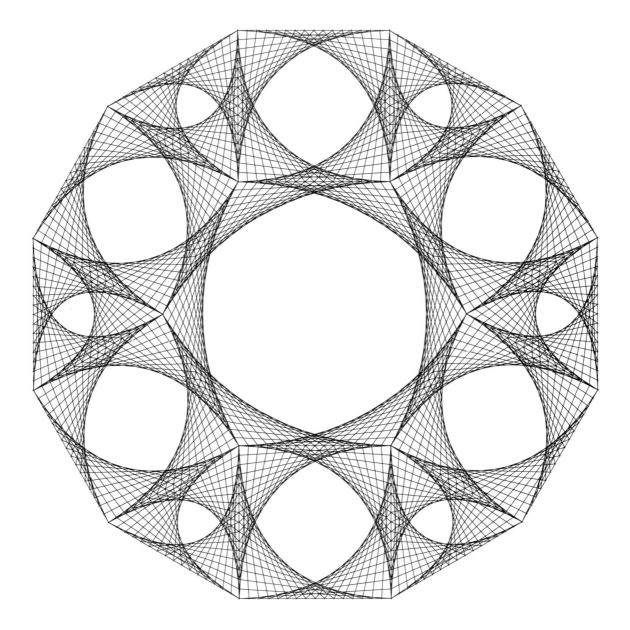

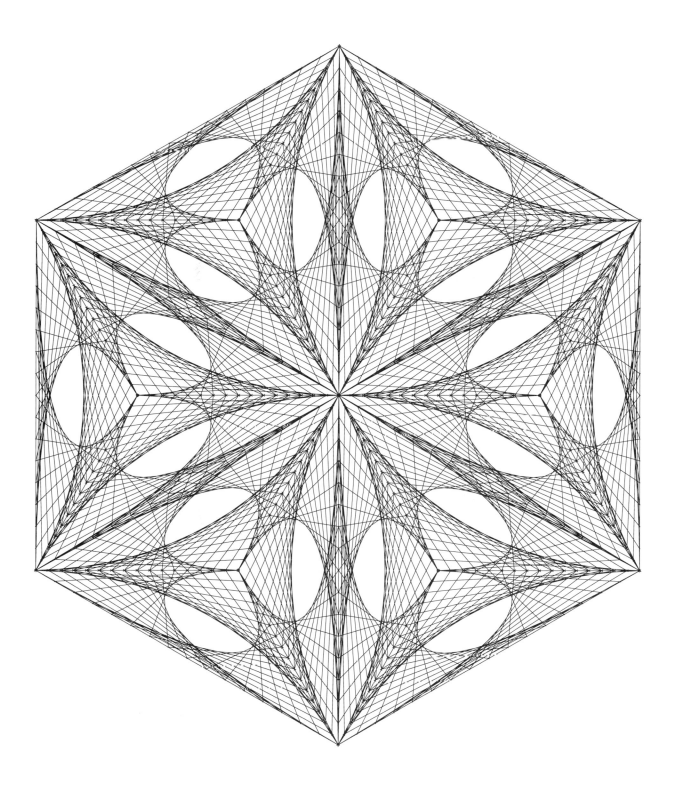

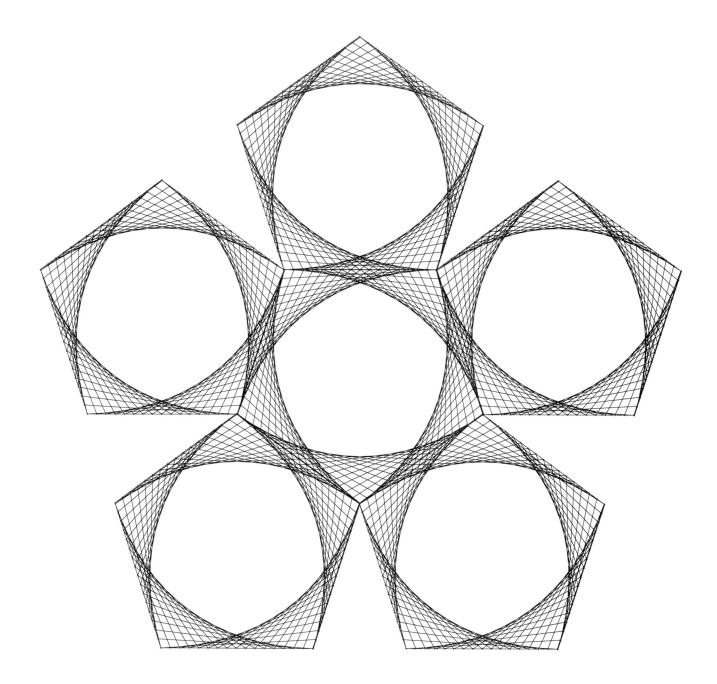

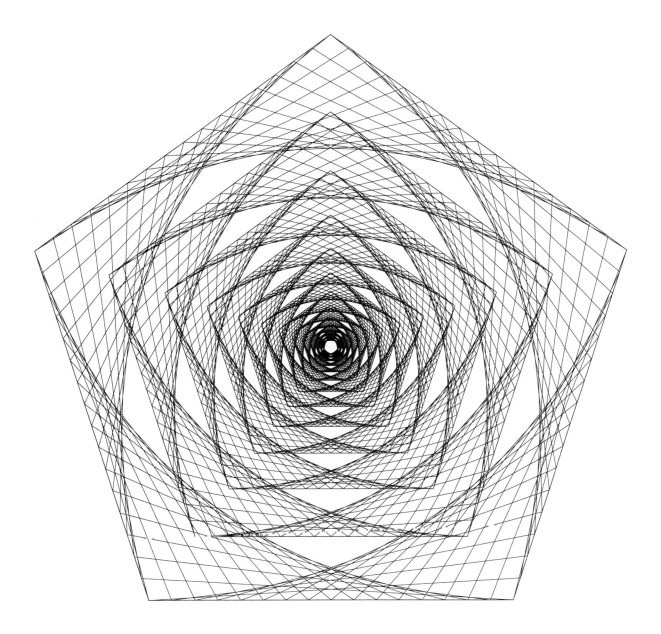

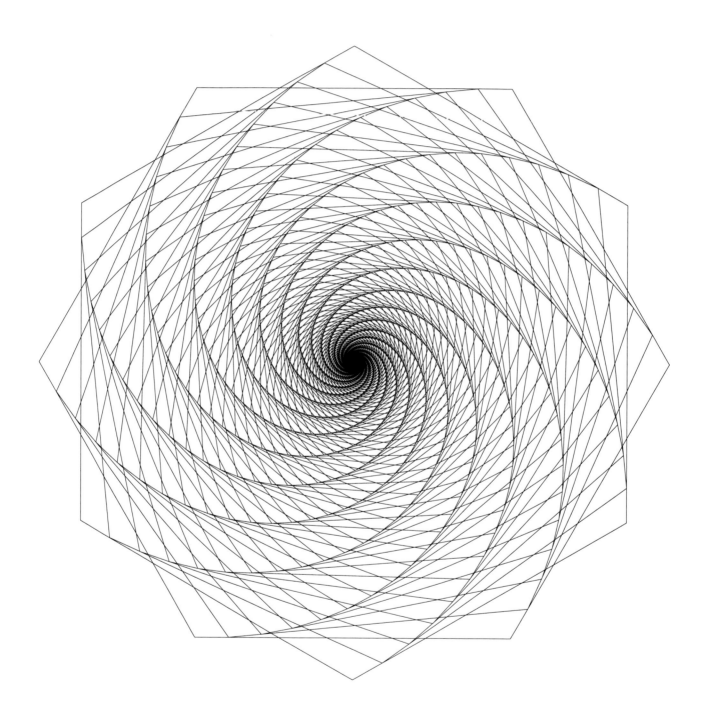

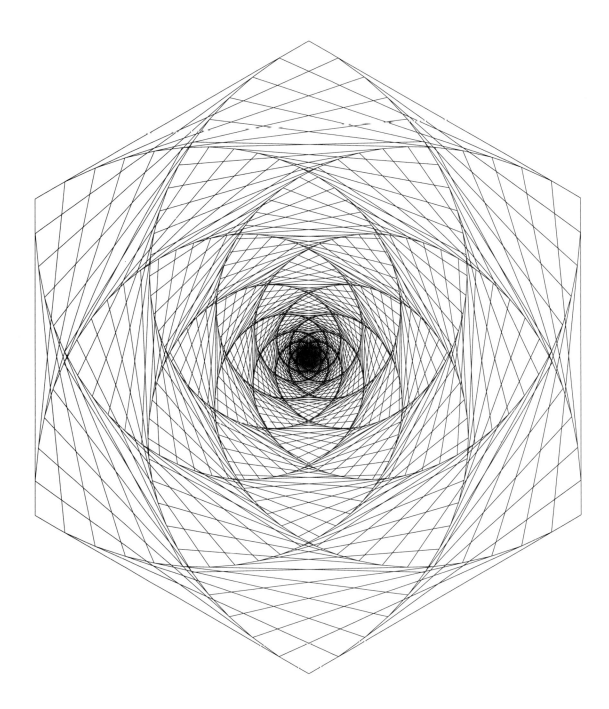

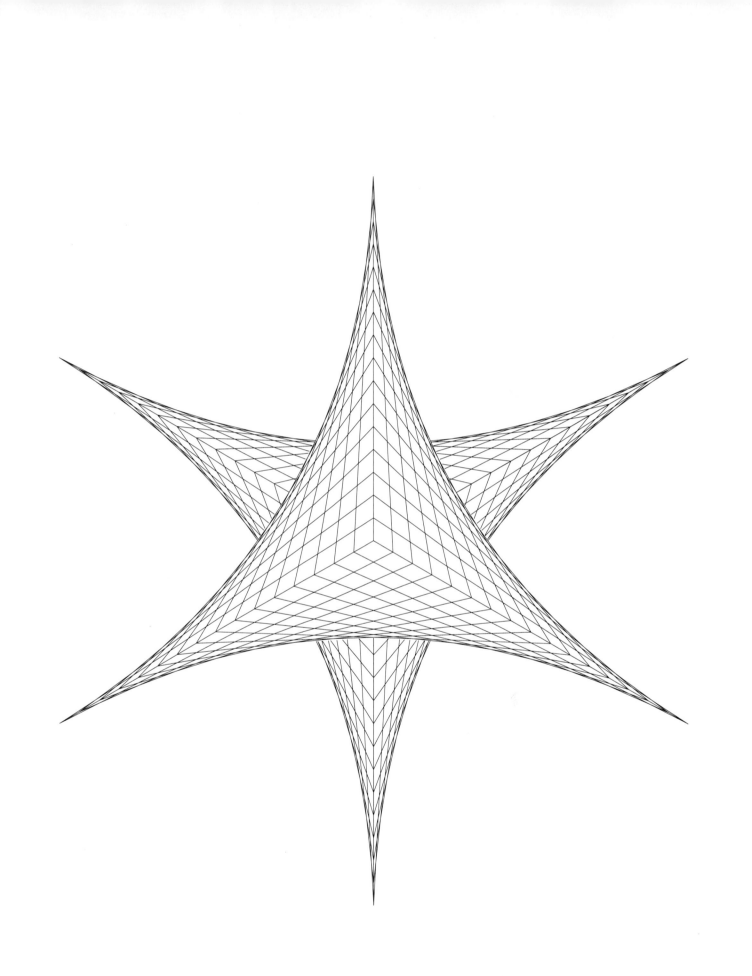

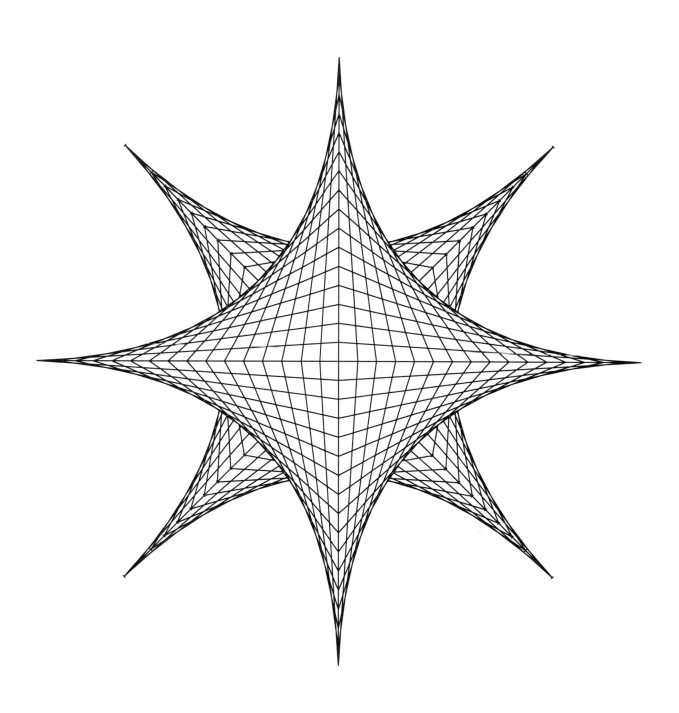

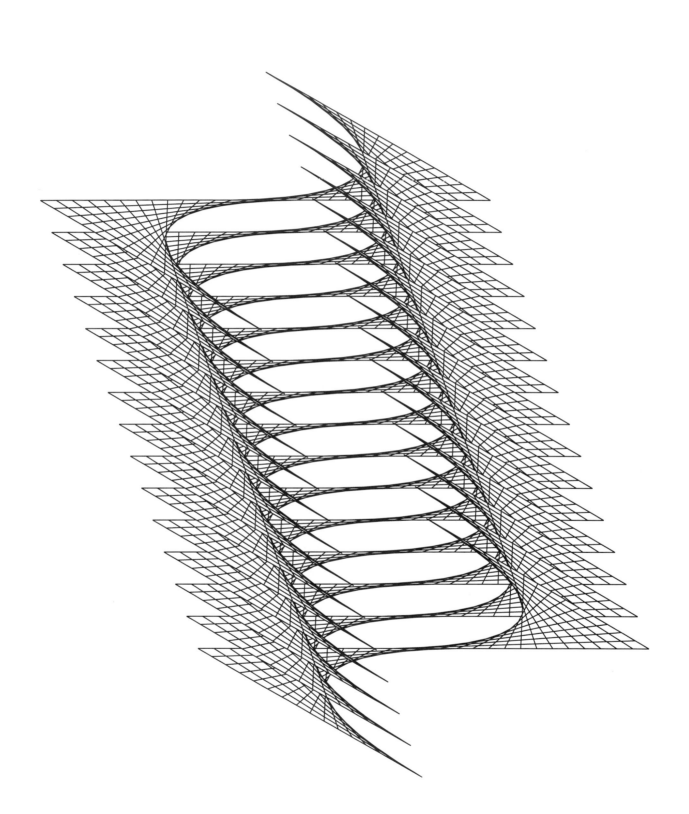

CHAPTER 8
DESIGN EFFECTS
FROM SHADING

This chapter shows how different visual effects can be created with line designs by coloring in selected sections of designs. Alternating sections can be filled with a solid black, grey, or color to create a striped or checkerboard effect. White on black designs also provide interesting variations of designs. Examples of white on black designs are shown in this chapter on pages 163–182. The only limitation to design possibilities is one's imagination.

LINE DESIGNS

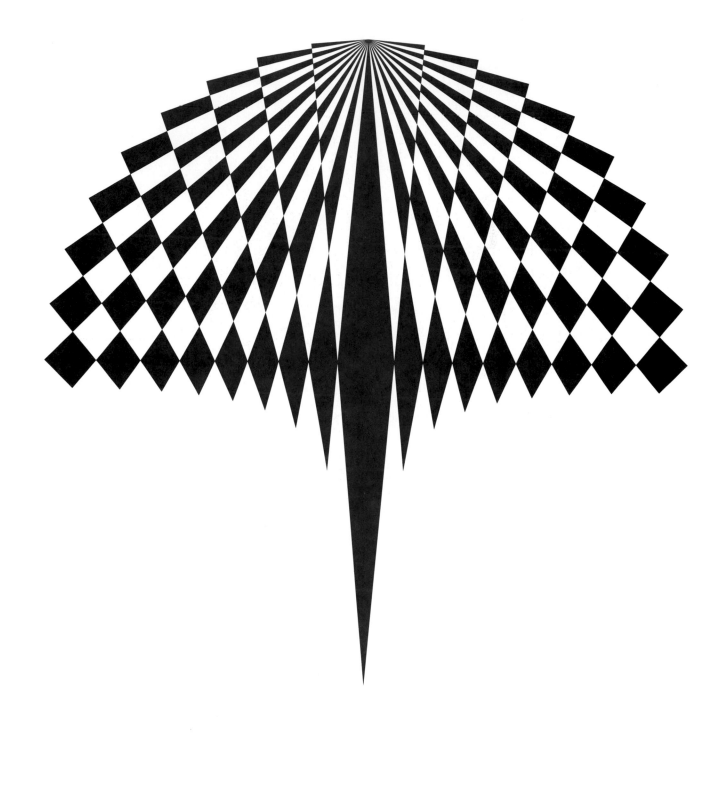

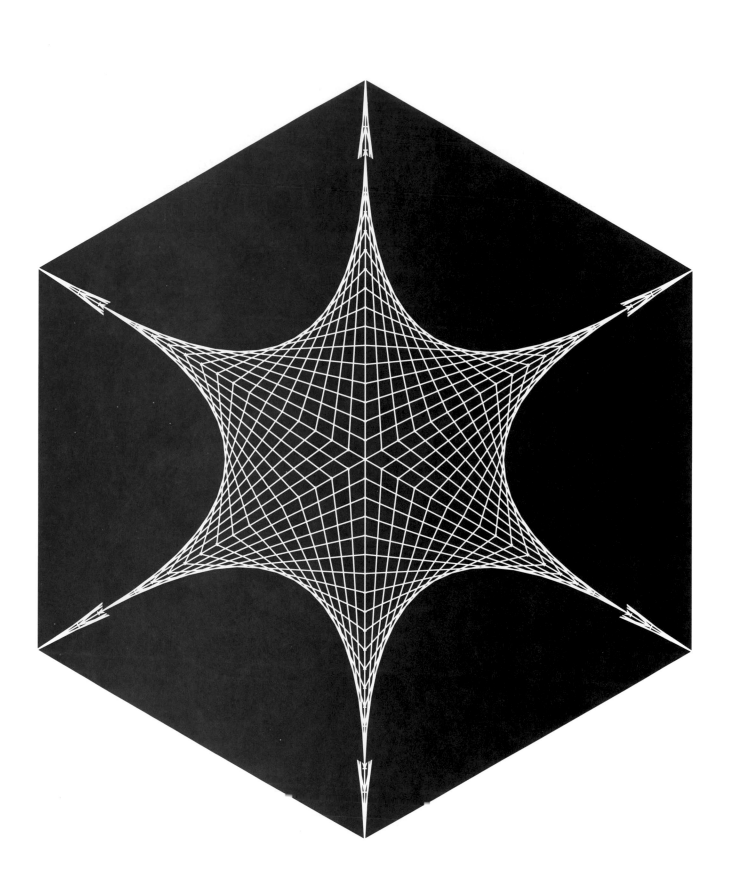

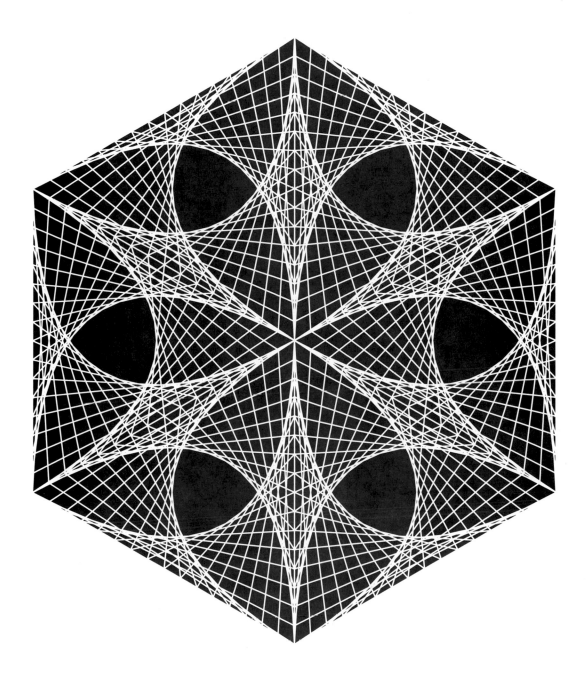

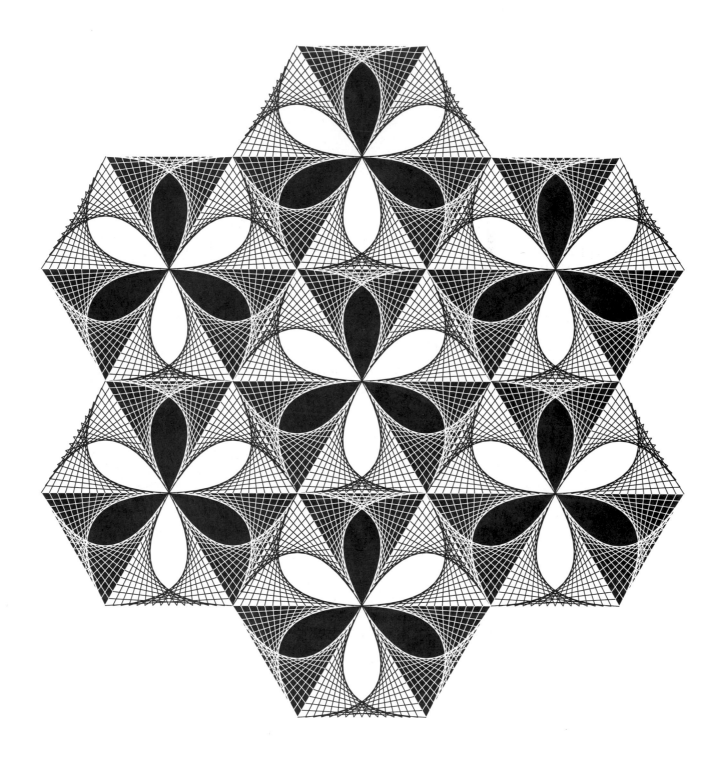

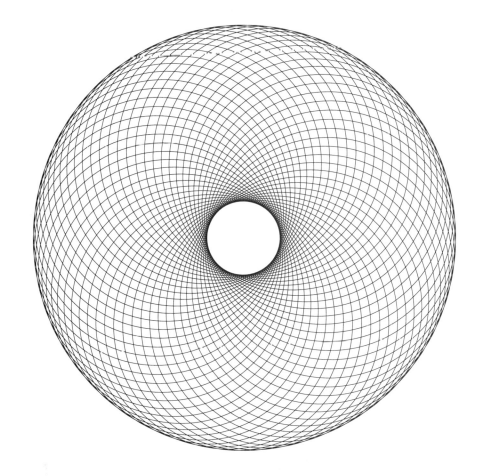

CHAPTER **9**

ROTATING
GEOMETRIC SHAPES

This chapter illustrates the various designs that can be generated by rotating a simple geometric object about a point in a plane. In nearly every case, some illusion of one or more circles will appear in the final result. As you can see, the size of the angle rotation also produces a variety of effects.

This type of design is a good example of the labor-saving capability of the personal computer. In most cases, drawing these designs with pencil, straightedge, or compass would present a laborious task.

This chapter is offered more for a visual exploration than for suggested activities.

Rotations of a Line Segment About a Point Not on the Segment

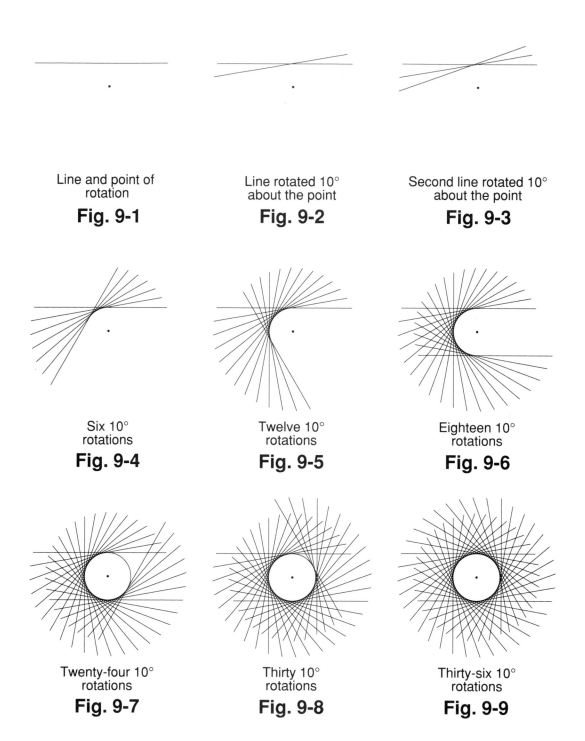

Line and point of rotation
Fig. 9-1

Line rotated 10° about the point
Fig. 9-2

Second line rotated 10° about the point
Fig. 9-3

Six 10° rotations
Fig. 9-4

Twelve 10° rotations
Fig. 9-5

Eighteen 10° rotations
Fig. 9-6

Twenty-four 10° rotations
Fig. 9-7

Thirty 10° rotations
Fig. 9-8

Thirty-six 10° rotations
Fig. 9-9

Rotations of a Line Segment About a Point Not on the Segment

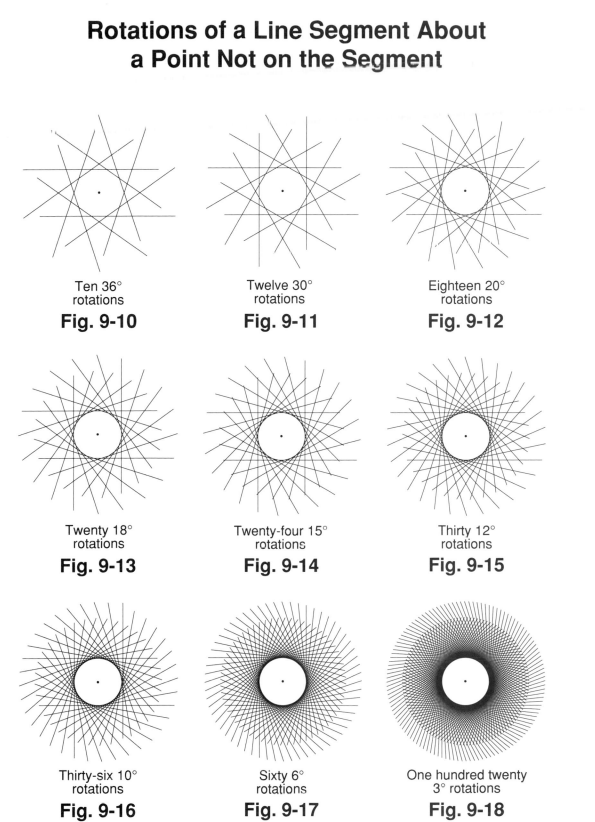

Ten 36°
rotations

Fig. 9-10

Twelve 30°
rotations

Fig. 9-11

Eighteen 20°
rotations

Fig. 9-12

Twenty 18°
rotations

Fig. 9-13

Twenty-four 15°
rotations

Fig. 9-14

Thirty 12°
rotations

Fig. 9-15

Thirty-six 10°
rotations

Fig. 9-16

Sixty 6°
rotations

Fig. 9-17

One hundred twenty
3° rotations

Fig. 9-18

Rotation of an Angle About
a Point Not on the Angle

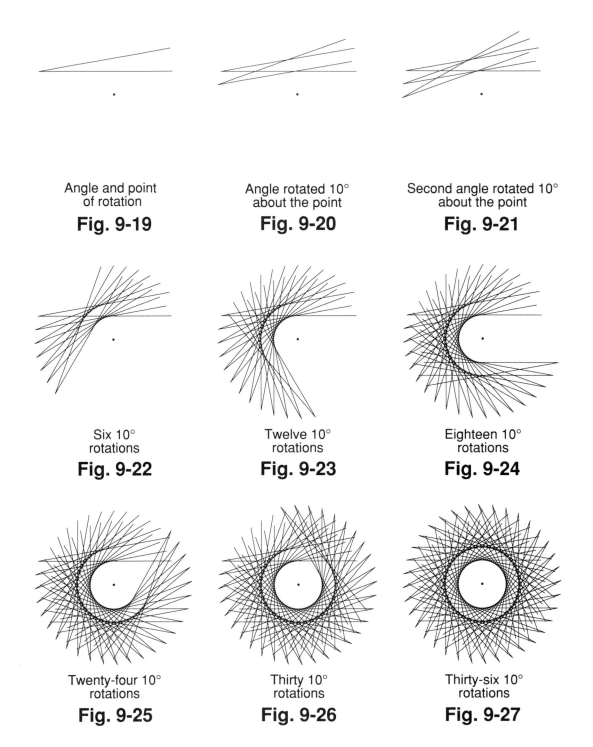

Angle and point
of rotation
Fig. 9-19

Angle rotated 10°
about the point
Fig. 9-20

Second angle rotated 10°
about the point
Fig. 9-21

Six 10°
rotations
Fig. 9-22

Twelve 10°
rotations
Fig. 9-23

Eighteen 10°
rotations
Fig. 9-24

Twenty-four 10°
rotations
Fig. 9-25

Thirty 10°
rotations
Fig. 9-26

Thirty-six 10°
rotations
Fig. 9-27

Rotations of an Angle About
a Point Not on the Angle

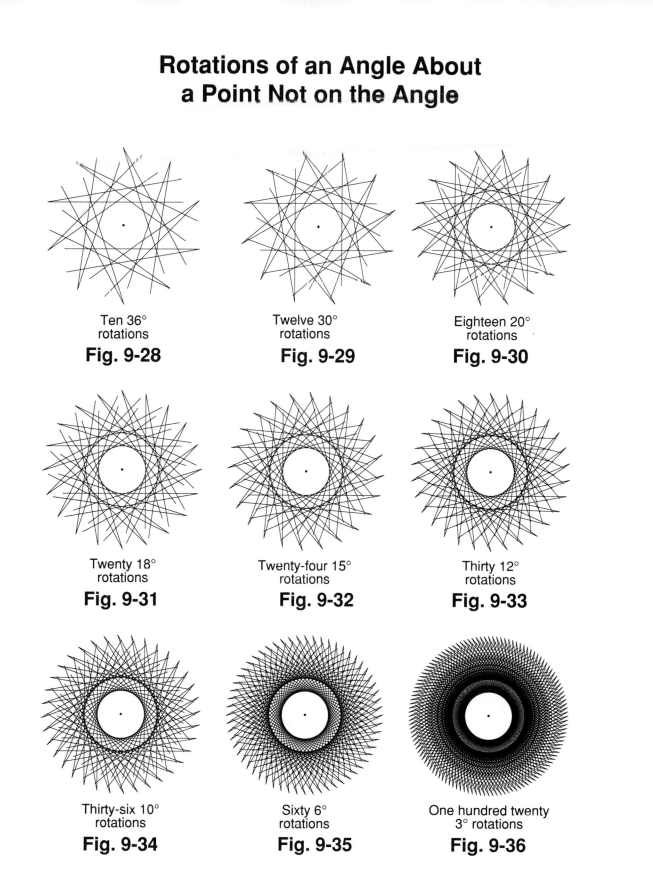

Ten 36°
rotations
Fig. 9-28

Twelve 30°
rotations
Fig. 9-29

Eighteen 20°
rotations
Fig. 9-30

Twenty 18°
rotations
Fig. 9-31

Twenty-four 15°
rotations
Fig. 9-32

Thirty 12°
rotations
Fig. 9-33

Thirty-six 10°
rotations
Fig. 9-34

Sixty 6°
rotations
Fig. 9-35

One hundred twenty
3° rotations
Fig. 9-36

Rotation of an Arc About
a Point Not on the Arc

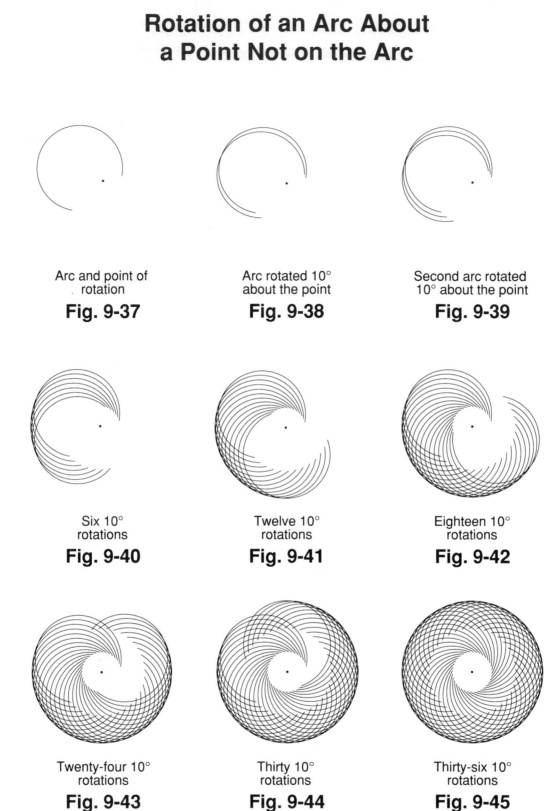

Arc and point of
rotation

Fig. 9-37

Arc rotated 10°
about the point

Fig. 9-38

Second arc rotated
10° about the point

Fig. 9-39

Six 10°
rotations

Fig. 9-40

Twelve 10°
rotations

Fig. 9-41

Eighteen 10°
rotations

Fig. 9-42

Twenty-four 10°
rotations

Fig. 9-43

Thirty 10°
rotations

Fig. 9-44

Thirty-six 10°
rotations

Fig. 9-45

Rotations of an Arc About
a Point Not on the Arc

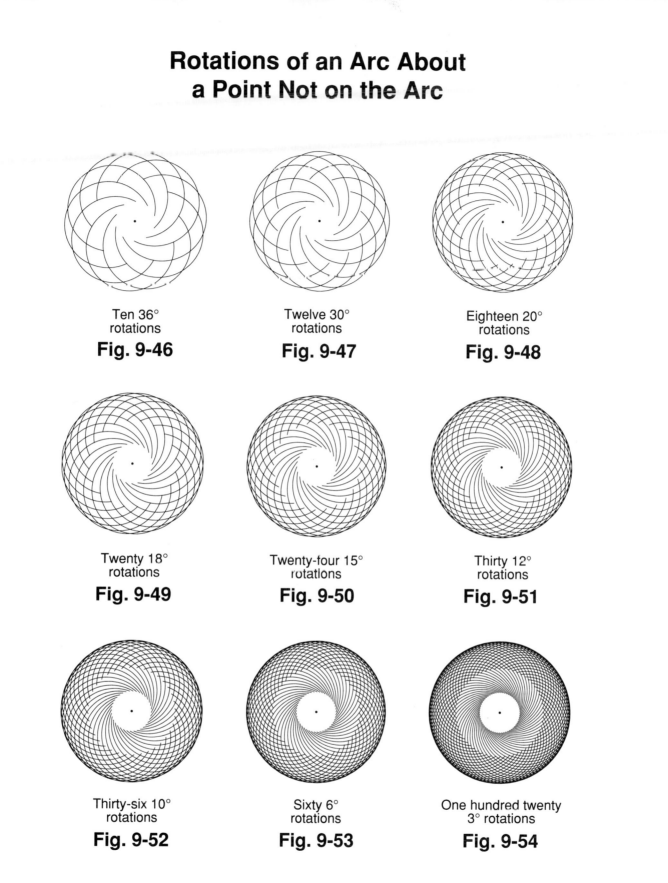

Ten 36°
rotations
Fig. 9-46

Twelve 30°
rotations
Fig. 9-47

Eighteen 20°
rotations
Fig. 9-48

Twenty 18°
rotations
Fig. 9-49

Twenty-four 15°
rotations
Fig. 9-50

Thirty 12°
rotations
Fig. 9-51

Thirty-six 10°
rotations
Fig. 9-52

Sixty 6°
rotations
Fig. 9-53

One hundred twenty
3° rotations
Fig. 9-54

Rotation of an Arc About
a Point on the Arc

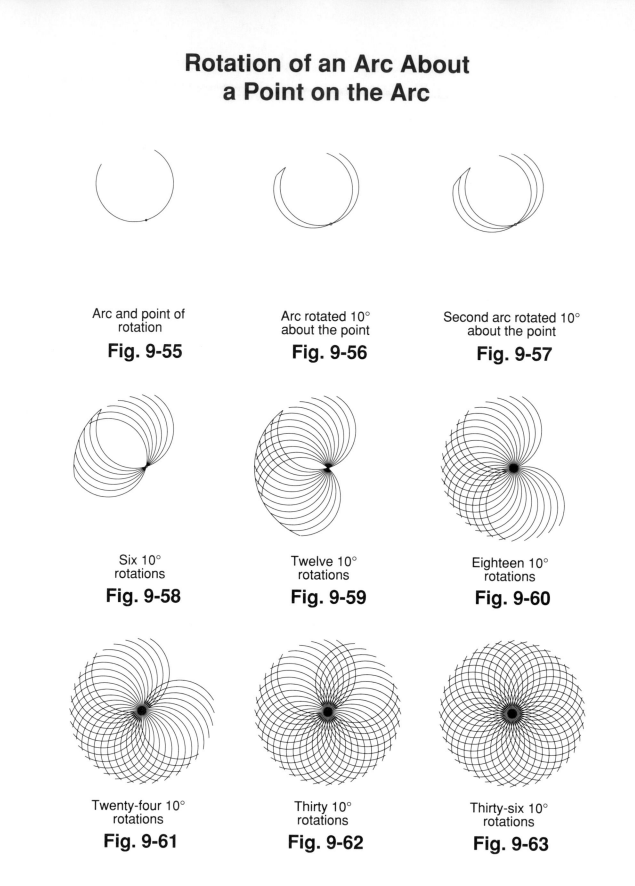

Arc and point of
rotation

Fig. 9-55

Arc rotated 10°
about the point

Fig. 9-56

Second arc rotated 10°
about the point

Fig. 9-57

Six 10°
rotations

Fig. 9-58

Twelve 10°
rotations

Fig. 9-59

Eighteen 10°
rotations

Fig. 9-60

Twenty-four 10°
rotations

Fig. 9-61

Thirty 10°
rotations

Fig. 9-62

Thirty-six 10°
rotations

Fig. 9-63

Rotations of an Arc About
a Point on the Arc

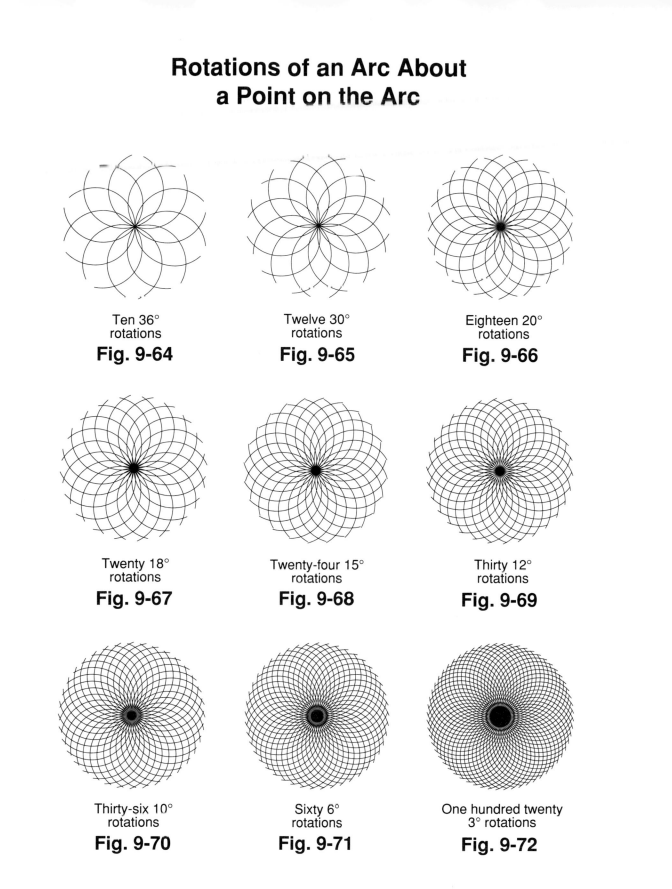

Ten 36°
rotations

Fig. 9-64

Twelve 30°
rotations

Fig. 9-65

Eighteen 20°
rotations

Fig. 9-66

Twenty 18°
rotations

Fig. 9-67

Twenty-four 15°
rotations

Fig. 9-68

Thirty 12°
rotations

Fig. 9-69

Thirty-six 10°
rotations

Fig. 9-70

Sixty 6°
rotations

Fig. 9-71

One hundred twenty
3° rotations

Fig. 9-72

Rotation of an Equilateral Triangle
About a Point Inside the Triangle

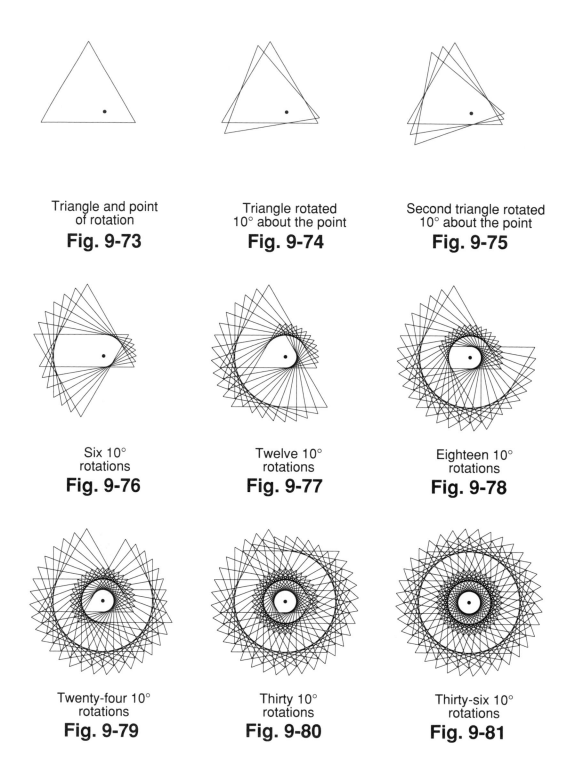

Triangle and point
of rotation
Fig. 9-73

Triangle rotated
10° about the point
Fig. 9-74

Second triangle rotated
10° about the point
Fig. 9-75

Six 10°
rotations
Fig. 9-76

Twelve 10°
rotations
Fig. 9-77

Eighteen 10°
rotations
Fig. 9-78

Twenty-four 10°
rotations
Fig. 9-79

Thirty 10°
rotations
Fig. 9-80

Thirty-six 10°
rotations
Fig. 9-81

Rotations of an Equilateral Triangle
About a Point Inside the Triangle

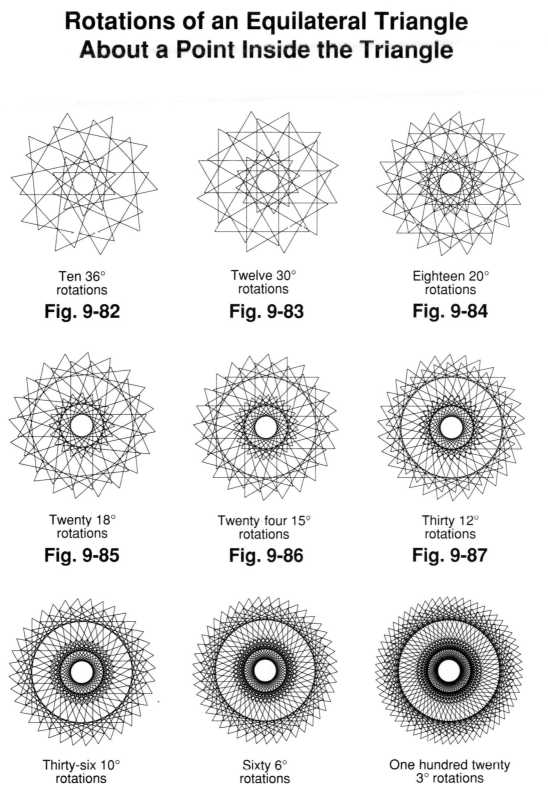

Ten 36°
rotations
Fig. 9-82

Twelve 30°
rotations
Fig. 9-83

Eighteen 20°
rotations
Fig. 9-84

Twenty 18°
rotations
Fig. 9-85

Twenty four 15°
rotations
Fig. 9-86

Thirty 12°
rotations
Fig. 9-87

Thirty-six 10°
rotations
Fig. 9-88

Sixty 6°
rotations
Fig. 9-89

One hundred twenty
3° rotations
Fig. 9-90

Rotations of Equilateral Triangles
About Their Centroid

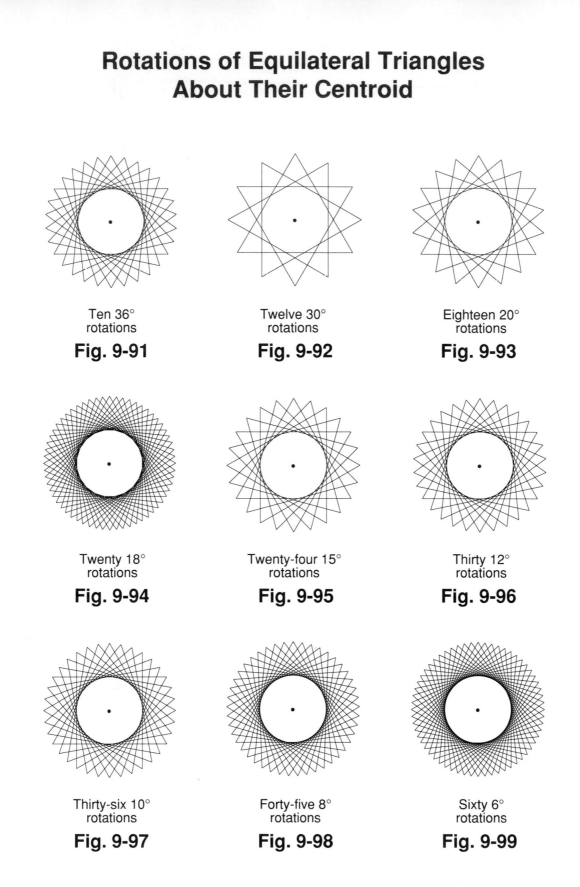

Ten 36°
rotations

Fig. 9-91

Twelve 30°
rotations

Fig. 9-92

Eighteen 20°
rotations

Fig. 9-93

Twenty 18°
rotations

Fig. 9-94

Twenty-four 15°
rotations

Fig. 9-95

Thirty 12°
rotations

Fig. 9-96

Thirty-six 10°
rotations

Fig. 9-97

Forty-five 8°
rotations

Fig. 9-98

Sixty 6°
rotations

Fig. 9-99

Rotations of Equilateral Triangles About a Point Outside the Triangle

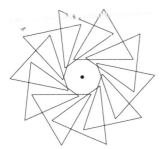

Ten 36°
rotations

Fig. 9-100

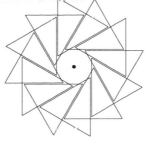

Twelve 30°
rotations

Fig. 9-101

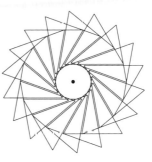

Eighteen 20°
rotations

Fig. 9-102

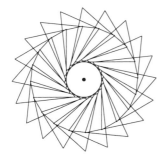

Twenty 18°
rotations

Fig. 9-103

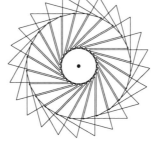

Twenty-four 15°
rotations

Fig. 9-104

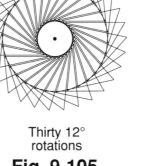

Thirty 12°
rotations

Fig. 9-105

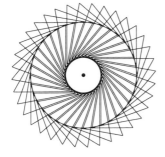

Thirty-six 10°
rotations

Fig. 9-106

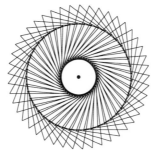

Forty-five 8°
rotations

Fig. 9-107

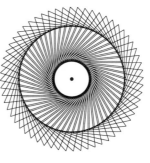

Sixty 6°
rotations

Fig. 9-108

Rotation of a Square About a Point Inside the Square

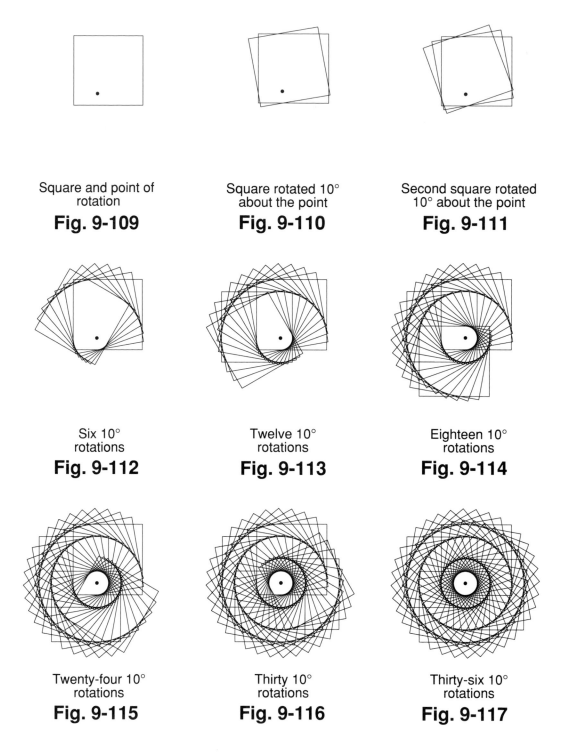

Square and point of rotation
Fig. 9-109

Square rotated 10° about the point
Fig. 9-110

Second square rotated 10° about the point
Fig. 9-111

Six 10° rotations
Fig. 9-112

Twelve 10° rotations
Fig. 9-113

Eighteen 10° rotations
Fig. 9-114

Twenty-four 10° rotations
Fig. 9-115

Thirty 10° rotations
Fig. 9-116

Thirty-six 10° rotations
Fig. 9-117

Rotations of a Square About a Point Inside the Square

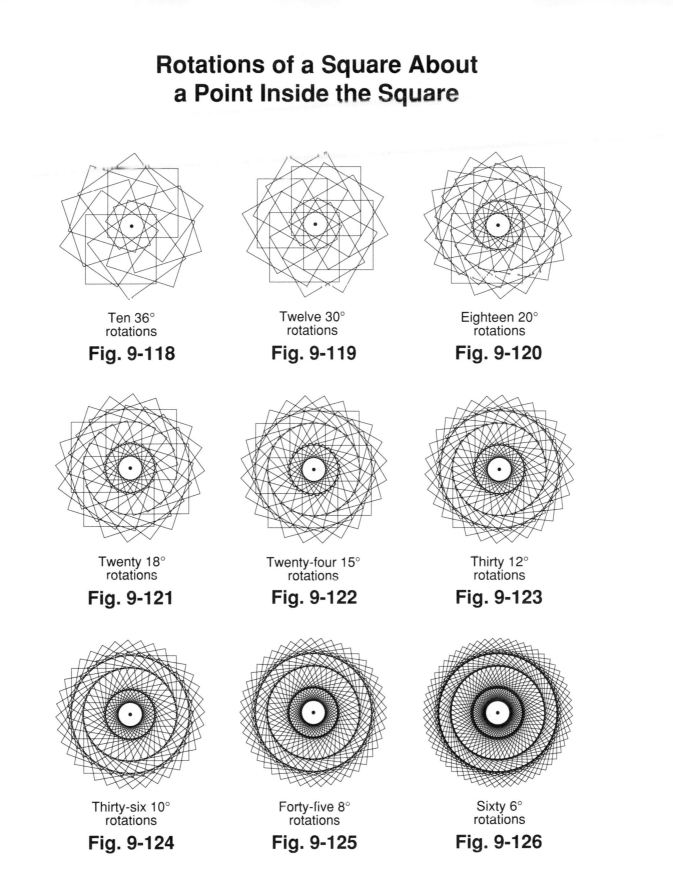

Ten 36°
rotations

Fig. 9-118

Twelve 30°
rotations

Fig. 9-119

Eighteen 20°
rotations

Fig. 9-120

Twenty 18°
rotations

Fig. 9-121

Twenty-four 15°
rotations

Fig. 9-122

Thirty 12°
rotations

Fig. 9-123

Thirty-six 10°
rotations

Fig. 9-124

Forty-five 8°
rotations

Fig. 9-125

Sixty 6°
rotations

Fig. 9-126

Rotations of a Square
About Its Centroid

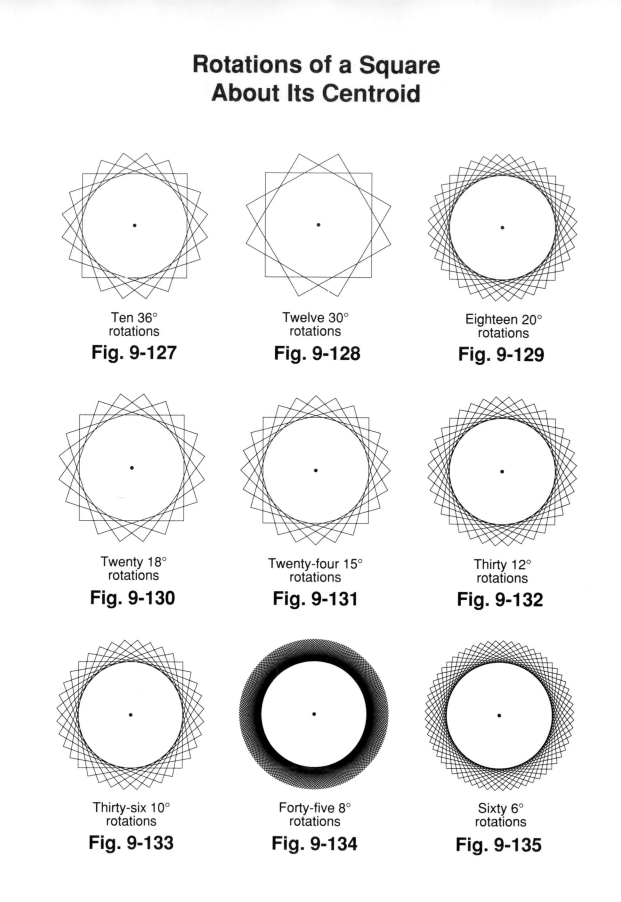

Ten 36°
rotations

Fig. 9-127

Twelve 30°
rotations

Fig. 9-128

Eighteen 20°
rotations

Fig. 9-129

Twenty 18°
rotations

Fig. 9-130

Twenty-four 15°
rotations

Fig. 9-131

Thirty 12°
rotations

Fig. 9-132

Thirty-six 10°
rotations

Fig. 9-133

Forty-five 8°
rotations

Fig. 9-134

Sixty 6°
rotations

Fig. 9-135

Rotation of a Circle About
a Point Inside the Circle

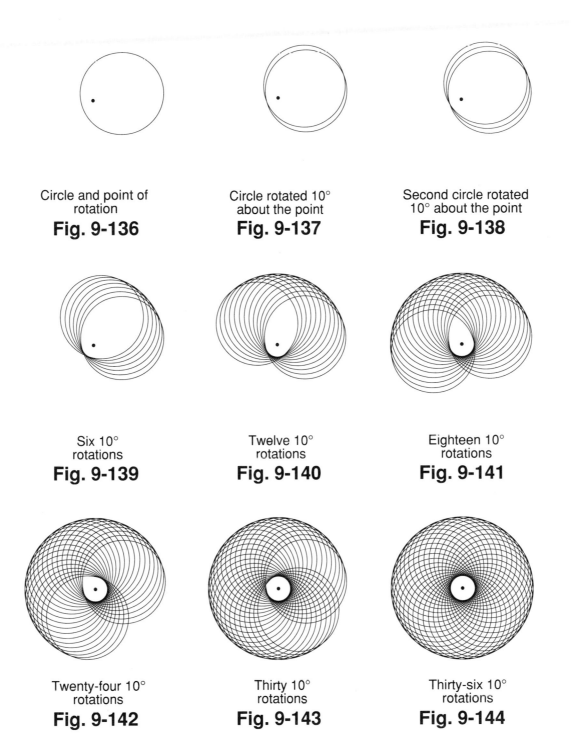

Circle and point of
rotation
Fig. 9-136

Circle rotated 10°
about the point
Fig. 9-137

Second circle rotated
10° about the point
Fig. 9-138

Six 10°
rotations
Fig. 9-139

Twelve 10°
rotations
Fig. 9-140

Eighteen 10°
rotations
Fig. 9-141

Twenty-four 10°
rotations
Fig. 9-142

Thirty 10°
rotations
Fig. 9-143

Thirty-six 10°
rotations
Fig. 9-144

Rotations of a Circle About a Point Inside the Circle

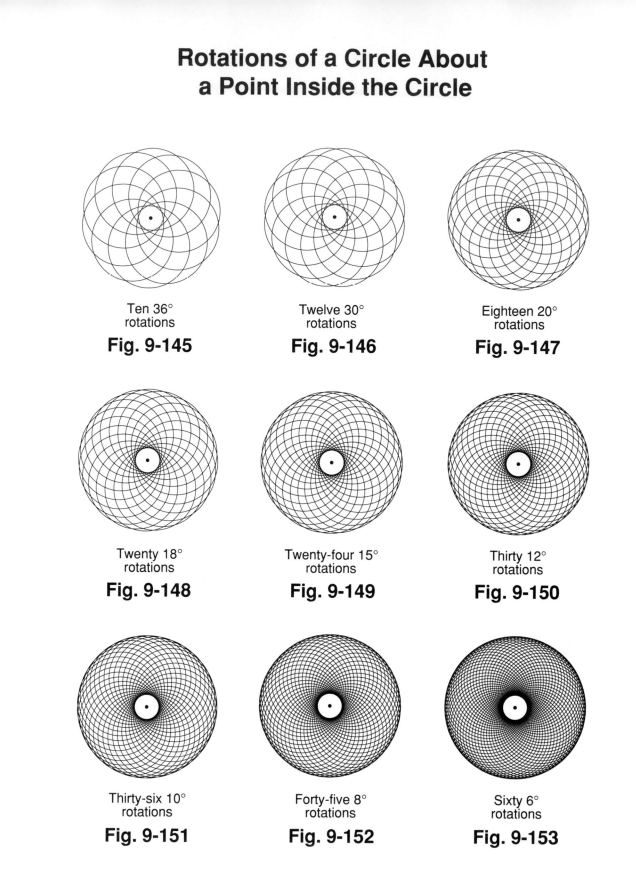

Ten 36°
rotations
Fig. 9-145

Twelve 30°
rotations
Fig. 9-146

Eighteen 20°
rotations
Fig. 9-147

Twenty 18°
rotations
Fig. 9-148

Twenty-four 15°
rotations
Fig. 9-149

Thirty 12°
rotations
Fig. 9-150

Thirty-six 10°
rotations
Fig. 9-151

Forty-five 8°
rotations
Fig. 9-152

Sixty 6°
rotations
Fig. 9-153

Rotations of a Circle About
a Point on the Circle

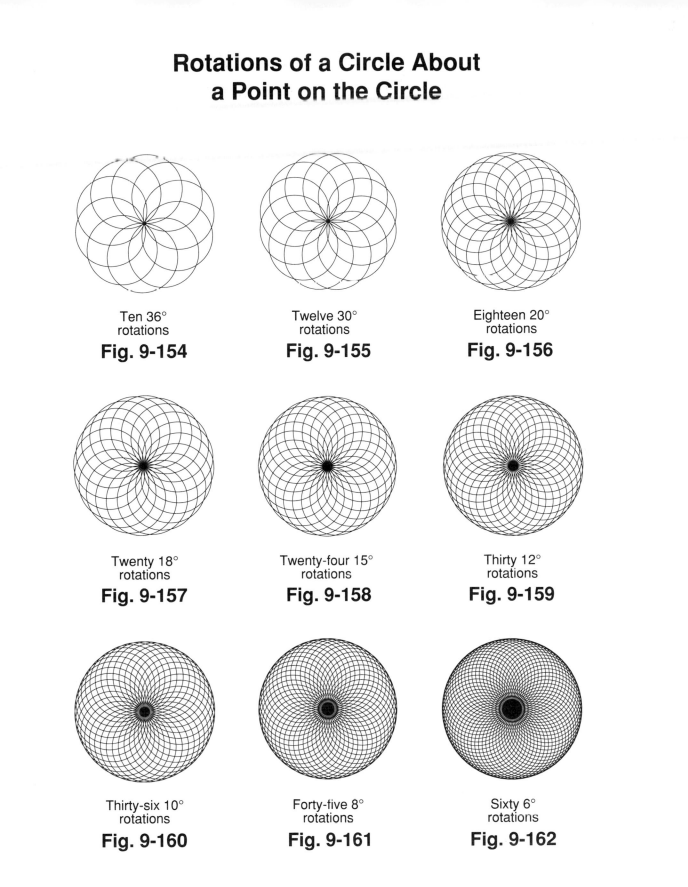

Ten 36°
rotations
Fig. 9-154

Twelve 30°
rotations
Fig. 9-155

Eighteen 20°
rotations
Fig. 9-156

Twenty 18°
rotations
Fig. 9-157

Twenty-four 15°
rotations
Fig. 9-158

Thirty 12°
rotations
Fig. 9-159

Thirty-six 10°
rotations
Fig. 9-160

Forty-five 8°
rotations
Fig. 9-161

Sixty 6°
rotations
Fig. 9-162

Rotation of an Ellipse About Its Center

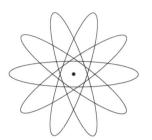

Ten 36°
rotations

Fig. 9-163

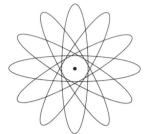

Twelve 30°
rotations

Fig. 9-164

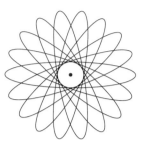

Eighteen 20°
rotations

Fig. 9-165

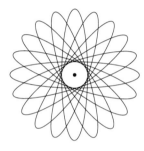

Twenty 18°
rotations

Fig. 9-166

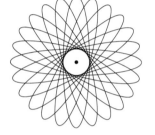

Twenty-four 15°
rotations

Fig. 9-167

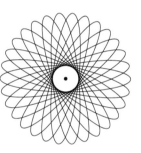

Thirty 12°
rotations

Fig. 9-168

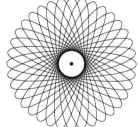

Thirty-six 10°
rotations

Fig. 9-169

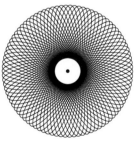

Forty-five 8°
rotations

Fig. 9-170

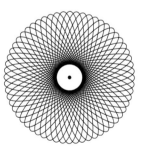

Sixty 6°
rotations

Fig. 9-171

10

COMBINING TECHNIQUES —GETTING CREATIVE

The designs shown in this chapter are designs created from other line designs or parts of line designs. Parts of line designs may serve as building blocks to create other designs. The example below shows how a series of inscribed triangles (Fig. 10-1) can be broken apart into a series of smaller elements (Fig. 10-2). Then one of these elements serves as a design element for a new design.

Fig. 10-3 shows the new design element taken from the original figure and rotated to a new vertical position. Fig. 10-4 shows the element reflected across a vertical axis. Fig. 10-5 shows the reflected element after it is rotated 60° five times.

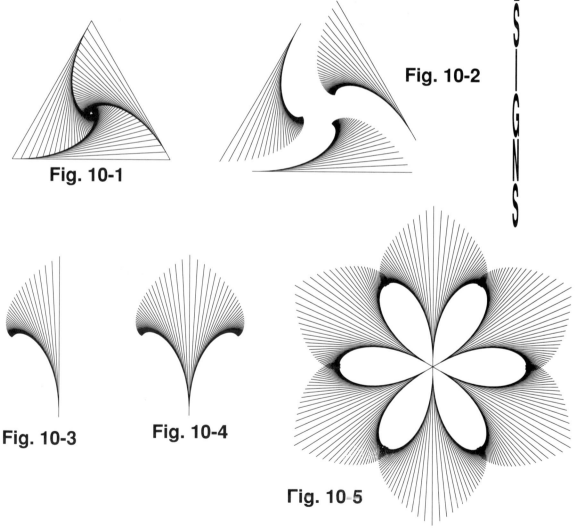

Fig. 10-1

Fig. 10-2

Fig. 10-3

Fig. 10-4

Fig. 10-5

Another detailed example similar to the example on the previous page is shown below. Fig. 10-6 begins with a design of squares inscribed in squares. Next, the four corner sections are separated. Fig. 10-8 shows one of the sections by itself, which is reflected in Fig. 10-9. The umbrella shape is rotated 90° three times about one of its points. The final figure shows the previous design rotated once 45°.

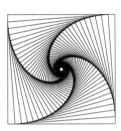

Fig. 10-6

Fig. 10-7

Fig. 10-8

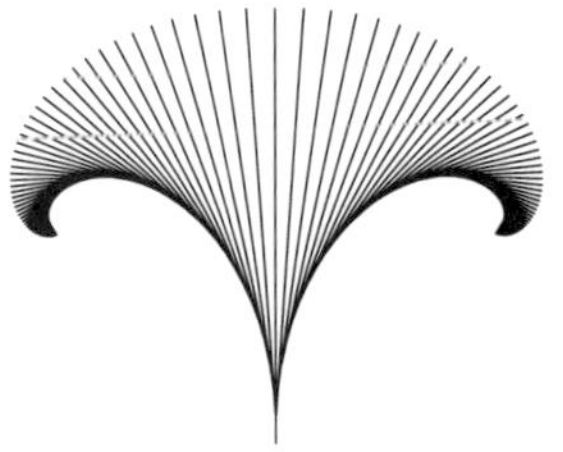

Fig. 10-9

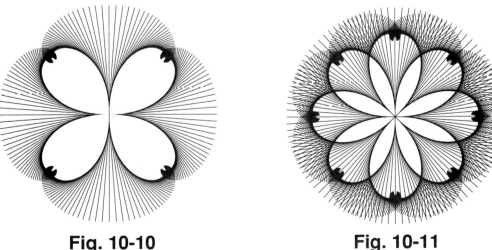

Fig. 10-10

Fig. 10-11

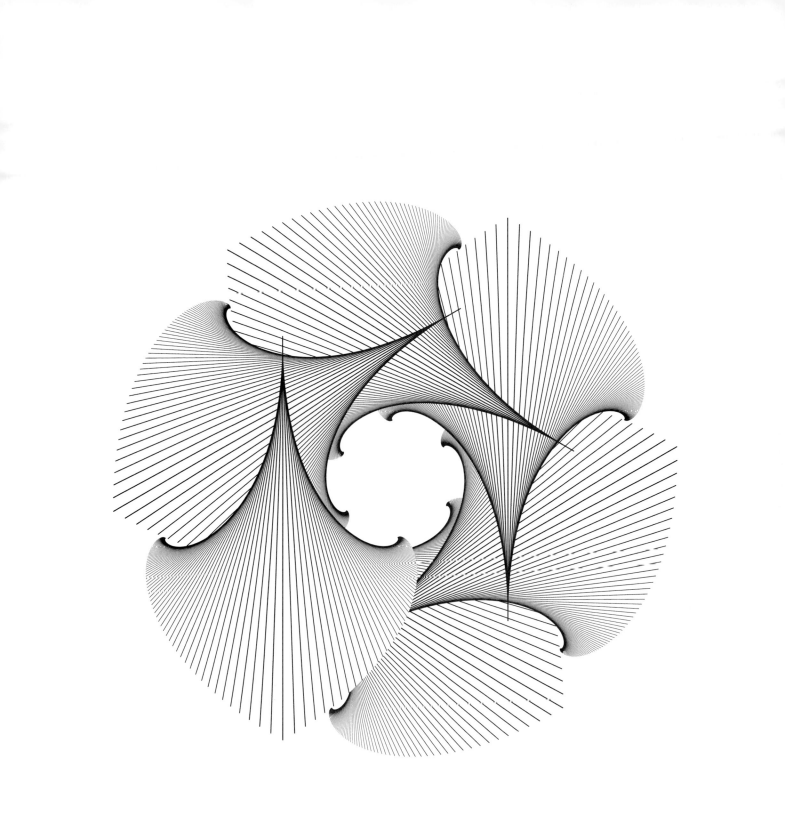

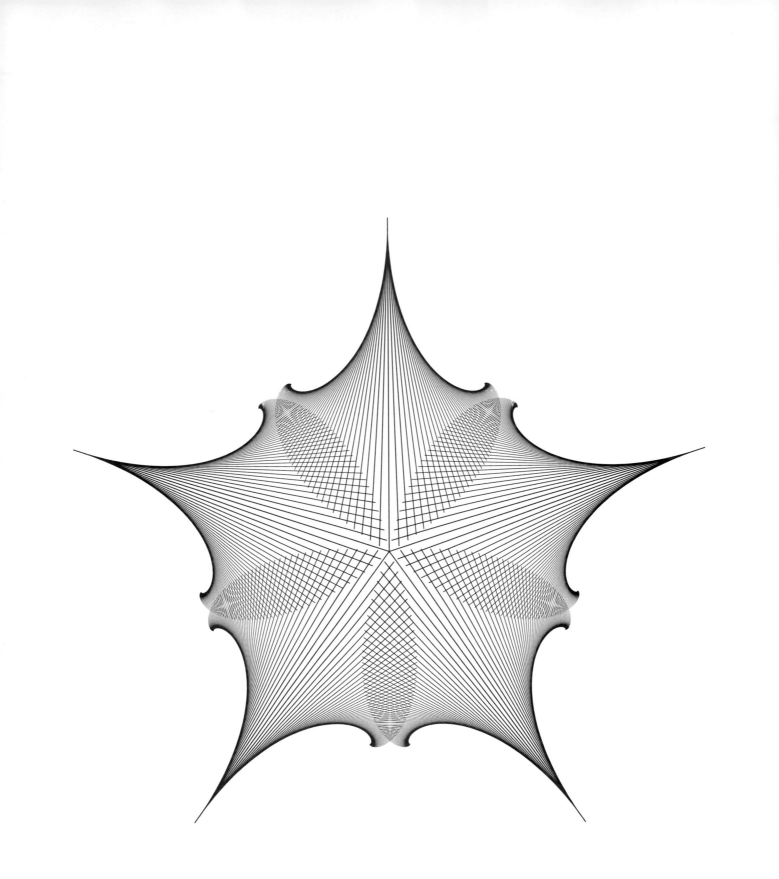

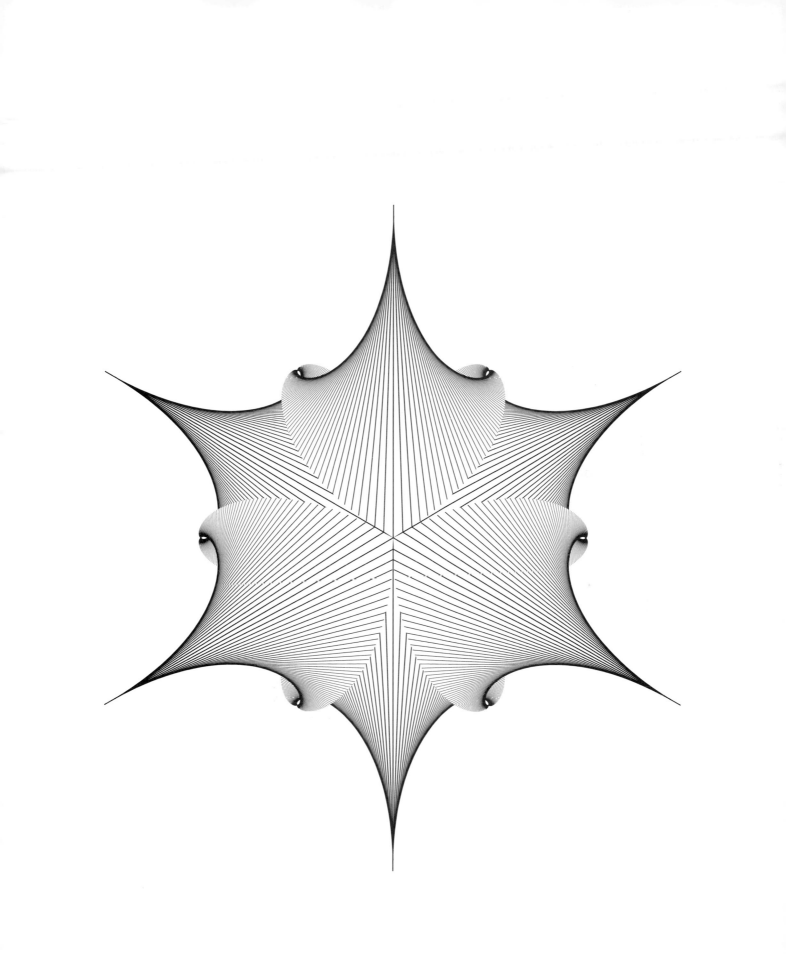

Slides, flips, and turns are geometric transformations. Often, slides are called translations, flips are called reflections, and turns are referred to as rotations. Two other transformations used in this book are reductions and enlargements.

Most personal computer drawing programs include the ability to reduce or enlarge diagrams. Figures 10-12 and 10-13, below, show reductions and enlargements of line designs.

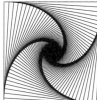

Design reduced 80%
Fig. 10-12

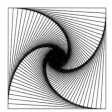 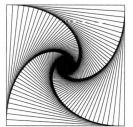

Design enlarged 120%
Fig. 10-13

Some programs allow for one transformation along the horizontal axis at the same time that a different transformation takes place along the vertical axis. Two examples of this are shown below:

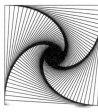 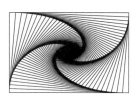 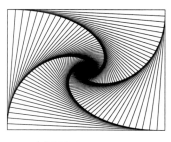

Original design
Fig. 10-14

120% horizontal
80% vertical
Fig. 10-15

160% horizontal
120% vertical
Fig. 10-16

Another transformation that is available on some computer drawing programs is a shear. When an object is sheared it may be thought of as being tilted. Its base and height, in one direction, remain constant, while other elements are stretched. The angle of shear and the axis along which the figure is sheared are the two necesary conditions of this transformation. Examples of sheared line designs are shown below:

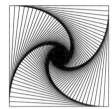 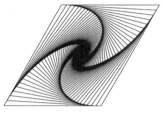

Shear of 30° along a horizontal axis
Fig. 10-17

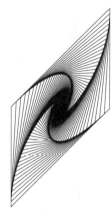

Shear of 45° along a vertical axis
Fig. 10-18

Shear of –60° along a horizontal axis
Fig. 10-19

Designs on several of the next few pages involve shears in their creation.

T he figures below show the step-by-step creation of the design shown on the opposite page.

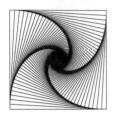

Inscribed squares
Fig. 10-20

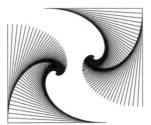

Design separated
Fig. 10-21

Left half of design
Fig. 10-22

50% vertical, 200% horizontal
Fig. 10-23

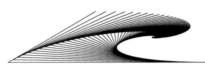

60° horizontal shear
Fig. 10-24

90°
rotation

Fig. 10-25

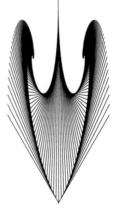

Reflection across
vertical axis

Fig. 10-26

L I N E   D E S I G N S

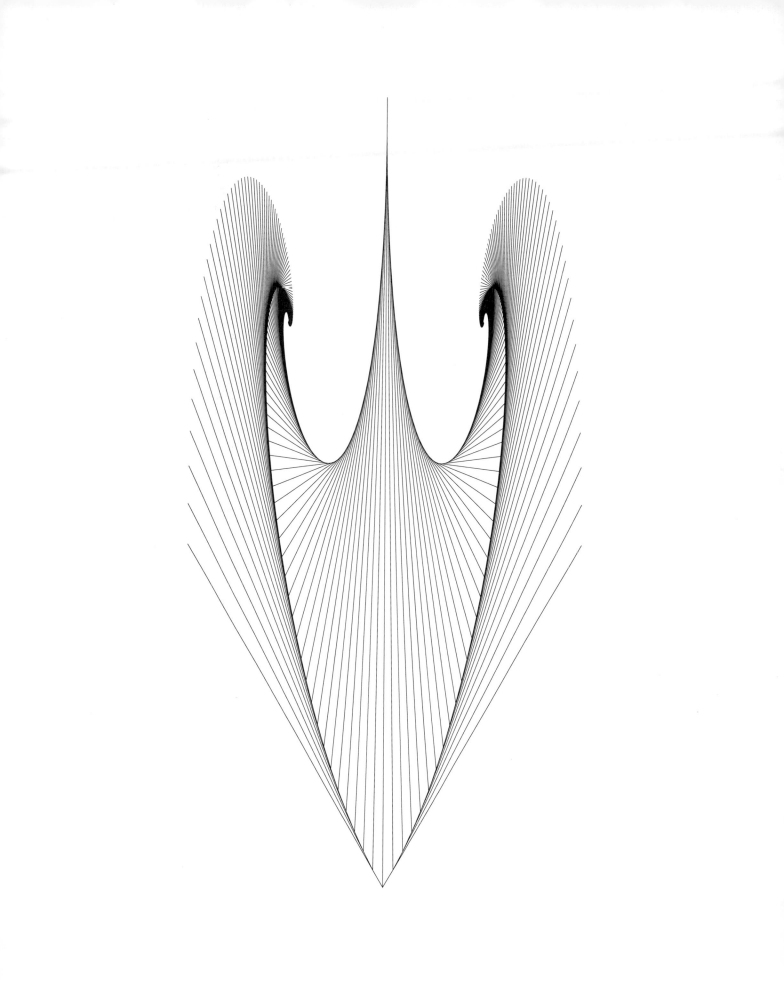

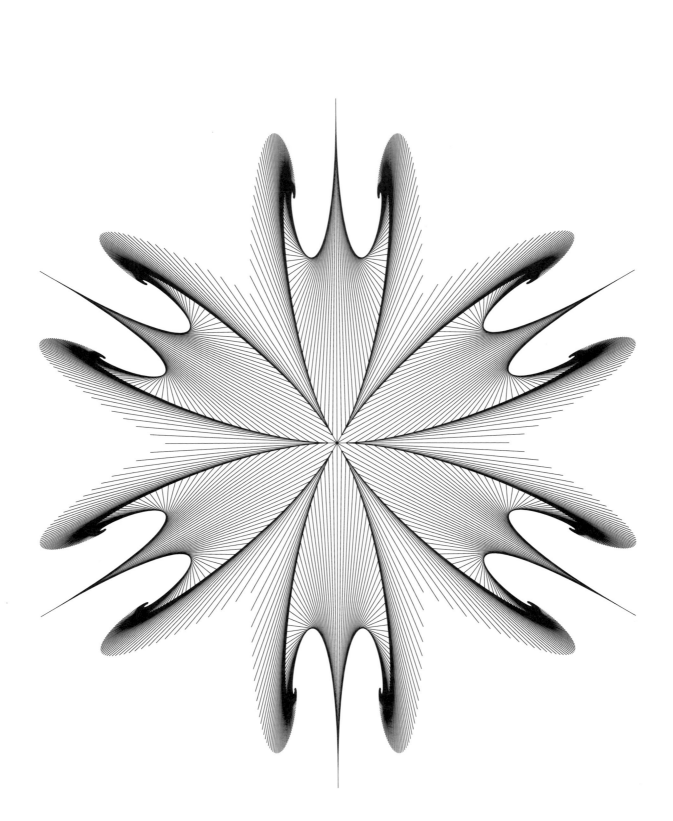

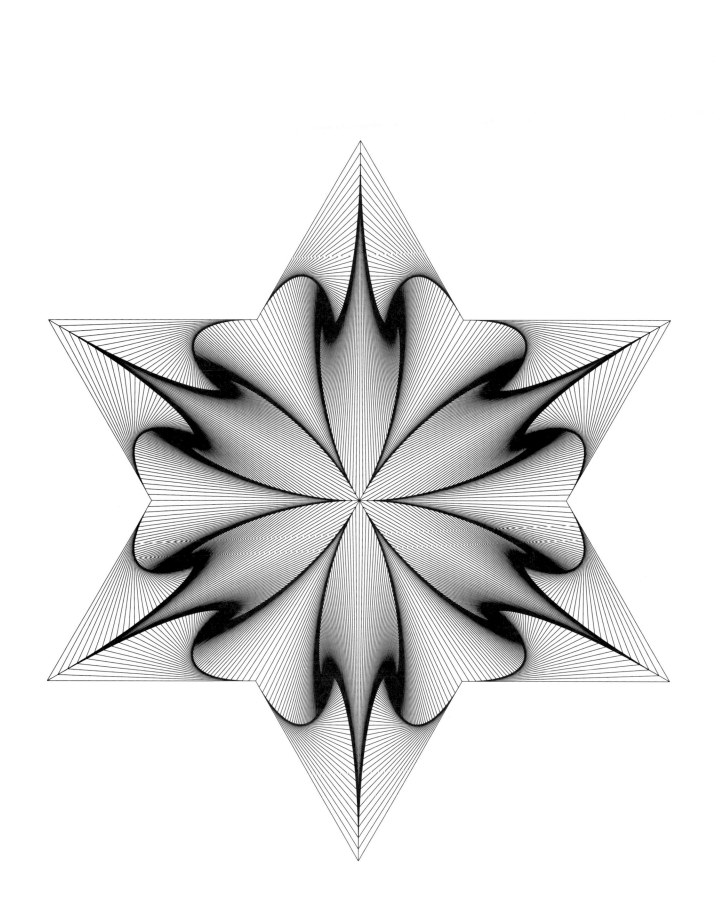

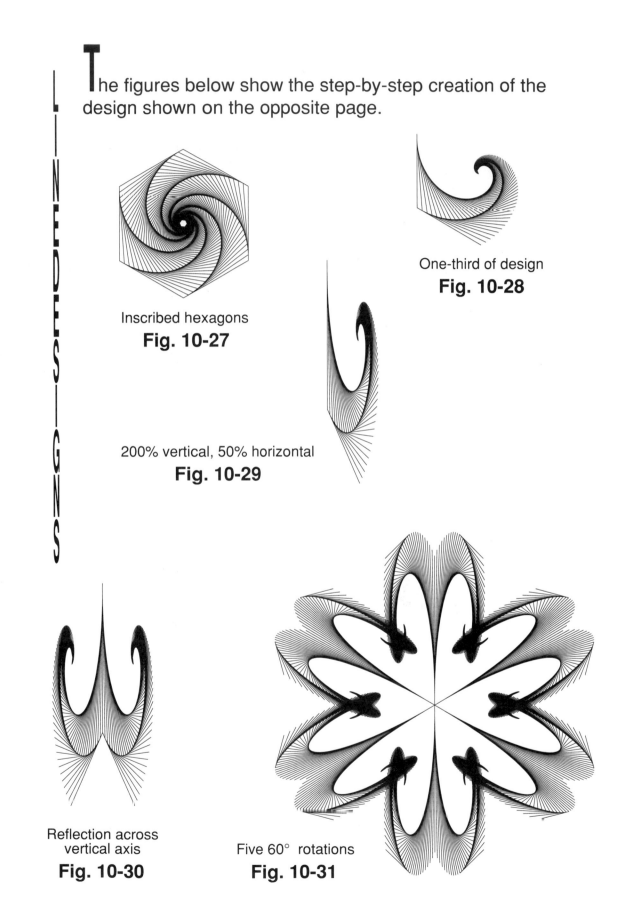

The figures below show the step-by-step creation of the design shown on the opposite page.

Inscribed hexagons
Fig. 10-27

One-third of design
Fig. 10-28

200% vertical, 50% horizontal
Fig. 10-29

Reflection across
vertical axis
Fig. 10-30

Five 60° rotations
Fig. 10-31

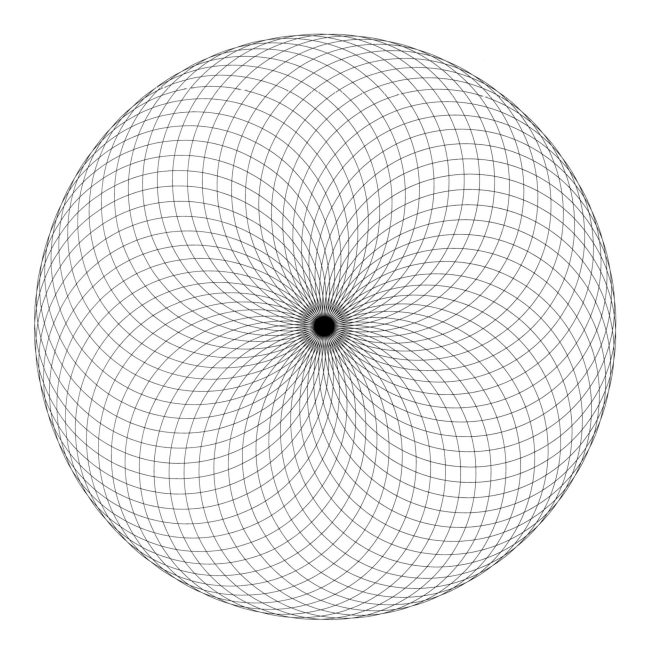

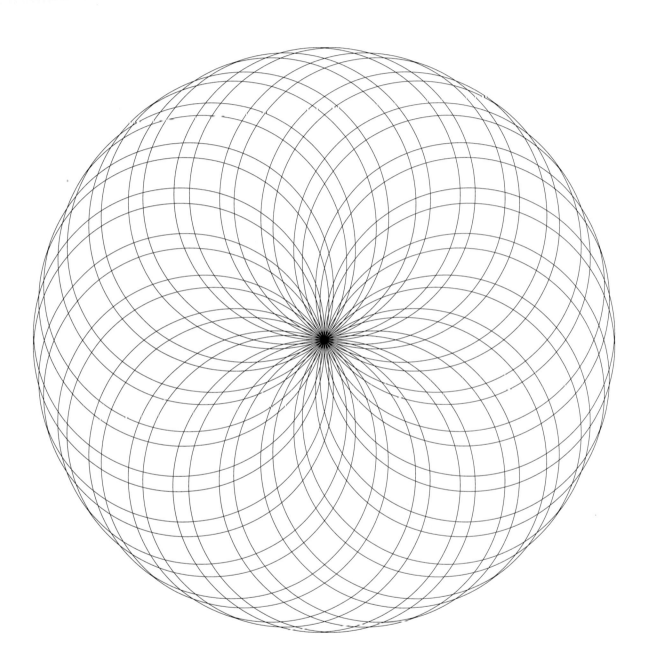

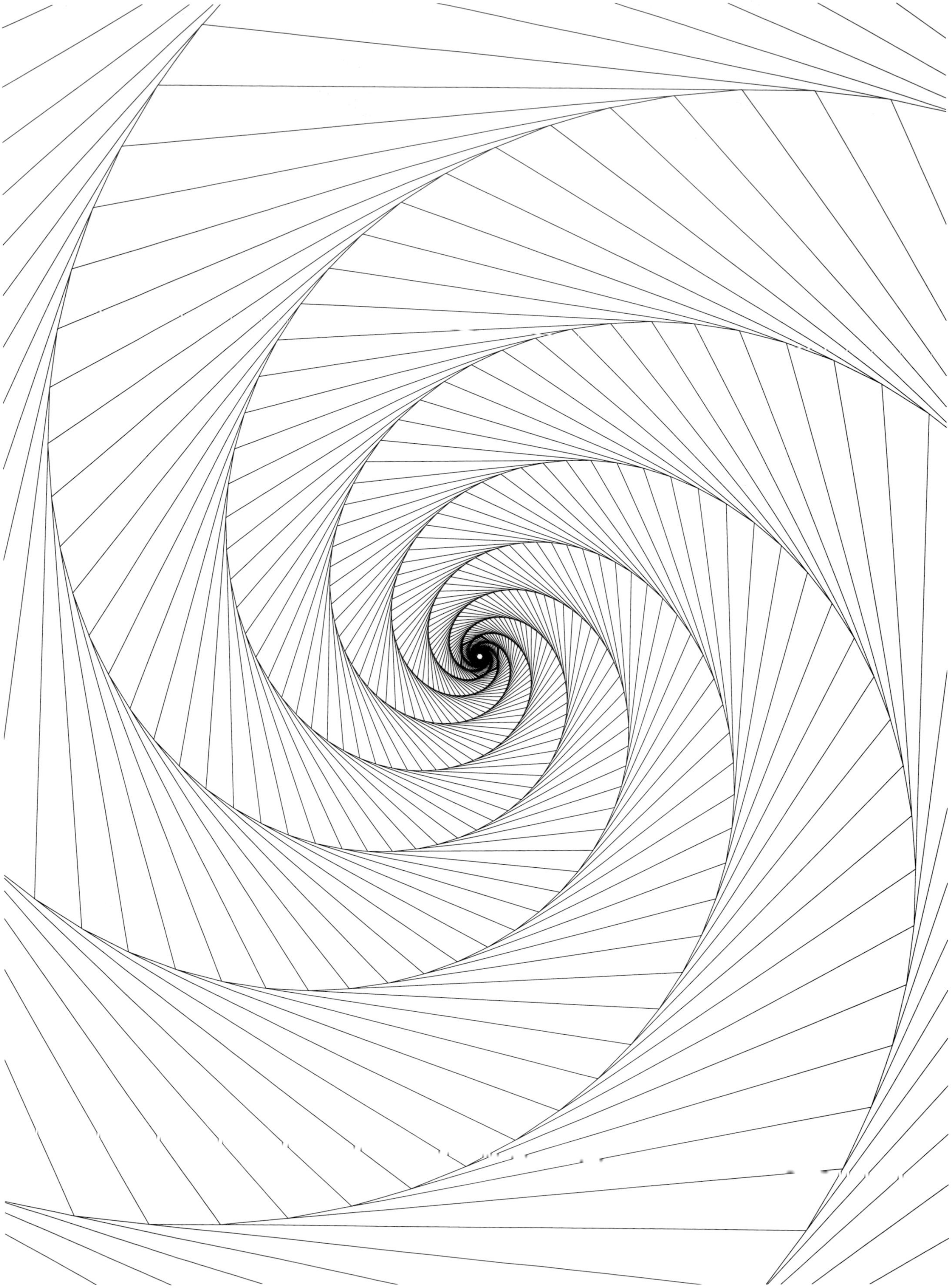

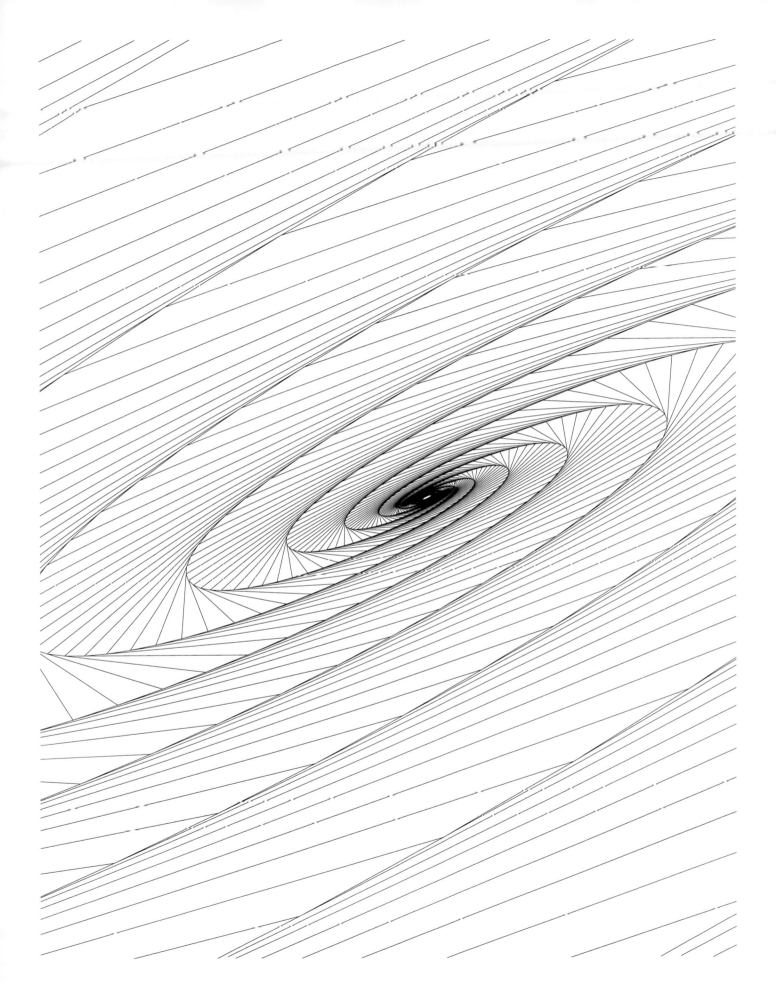

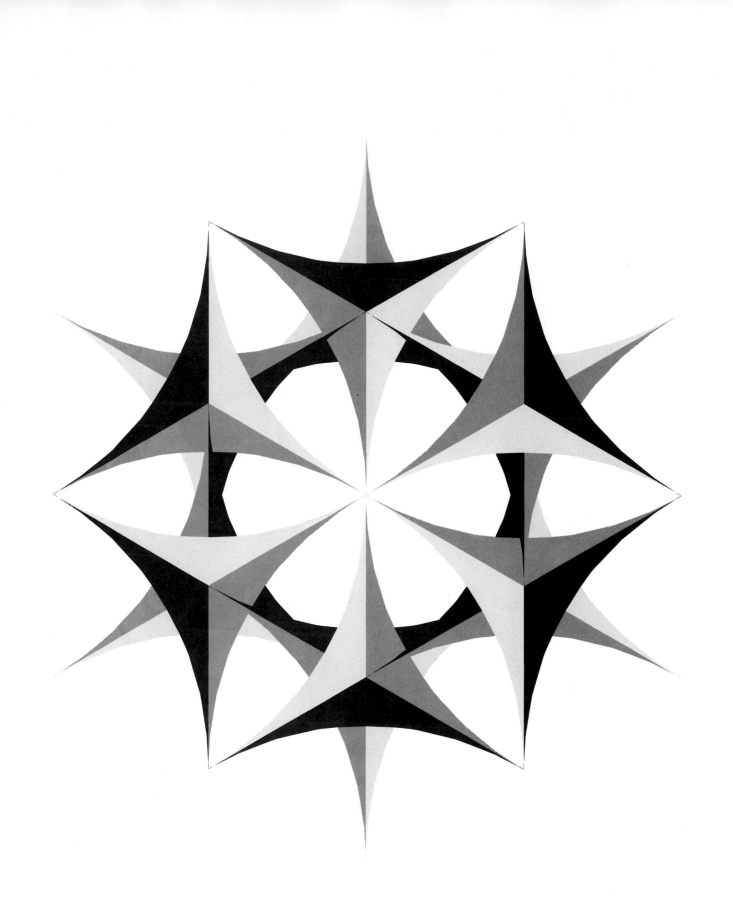

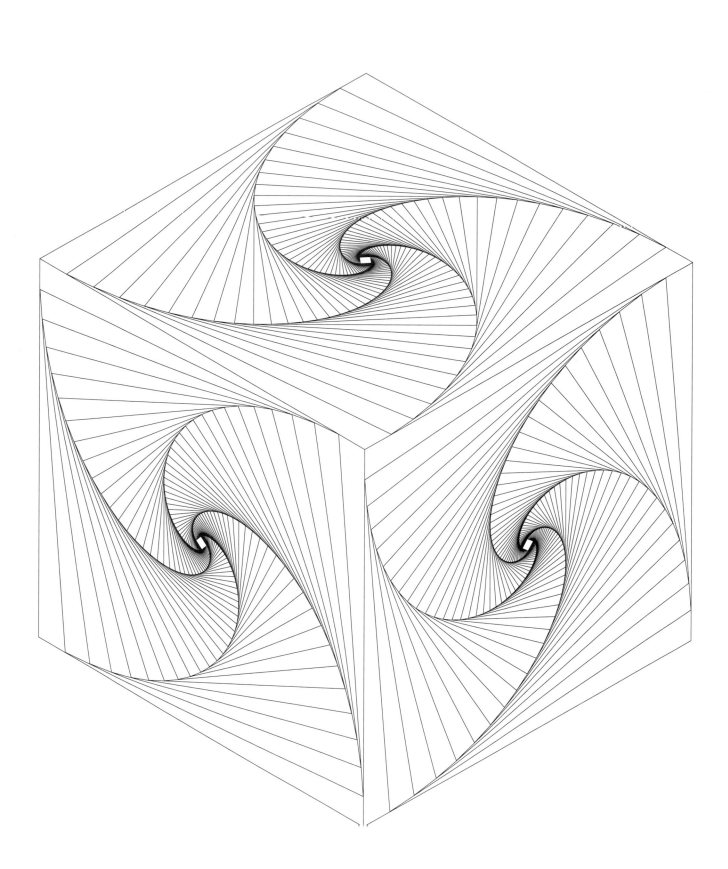

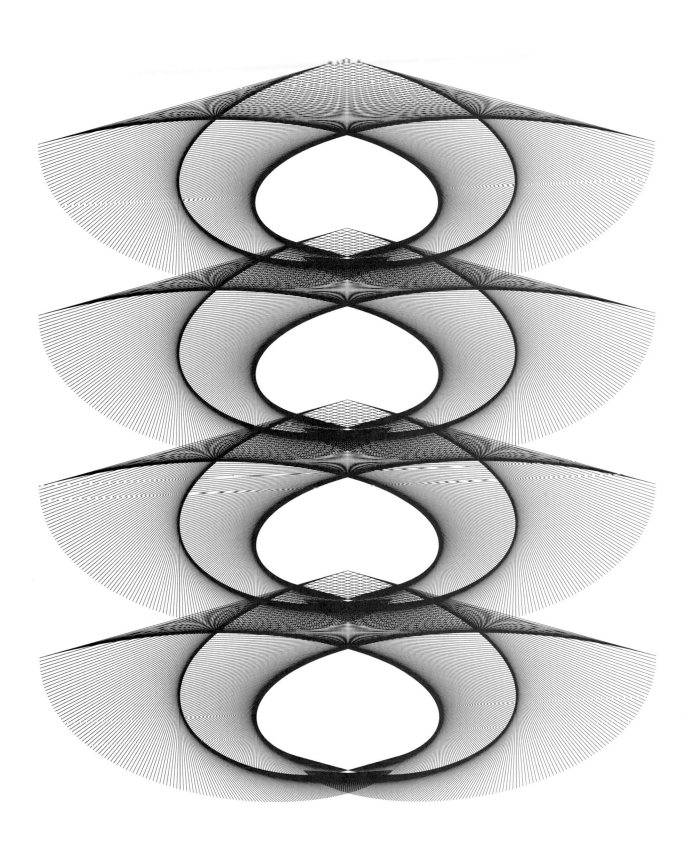

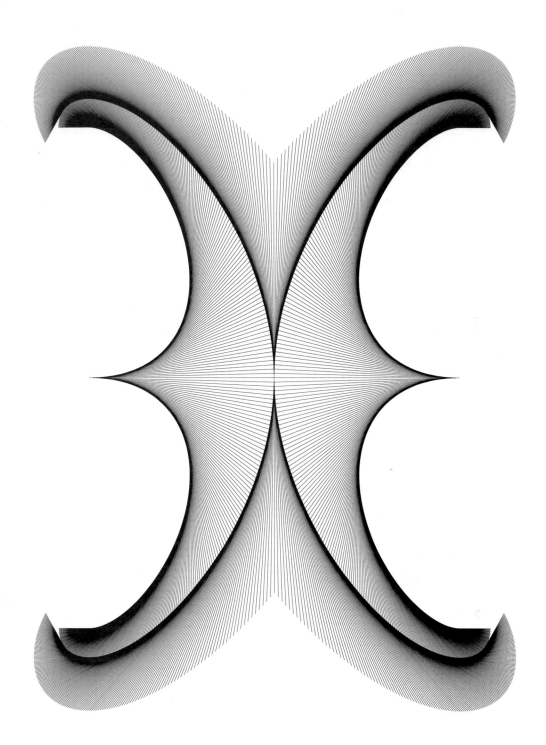

Chapter 10: Combining Techniques—Getting Creative **243**

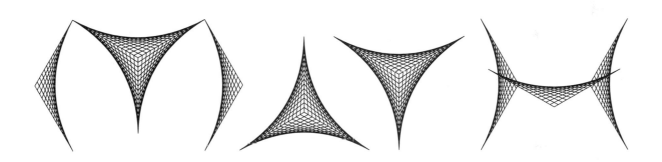

CHAPTER **11**

MATHEMATICAL
RELATIONSHIPS

Most of the curve illusions created by the line designs in this book have the shape of a parabola, an ellipse, or a circle. All of these shapes are defined as *conics*. They are called conics or conic sections since they can be taken as sections of a right circular cone. The illustrations on the opposite page show examples of cones or double cones that are sliced by planes of various orientations.

A cone could be imagined as an infinite stack of successively smaller or larger circles. A slice of a cone perpendicular to its axis will always result in a circle as a cross section. A parabola is created by a plane parallel to the slant height of the cone. An ellipse is formed by a plane cutting the cone at an oblique angle. Finally, a hyperbola is formed when a plane cuts the cone parallel to its axis. A hyperbola has two elements since it is the only conic that can intersect both parts of a double cone.

Each of these conic sections contains many special mathematical properties and real-world applications. It is not the purpose of this book to discuss those properties in any detail. It is, however, important to realize that the curves in the designs in this book are definable. It is also interesting to observe the interrelationships of various conics in the ways that they can be generated by line designs.

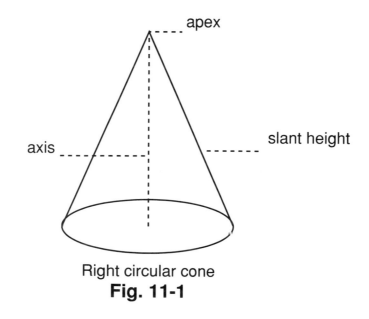

Right circular cone
Fig. 11-1

Conics

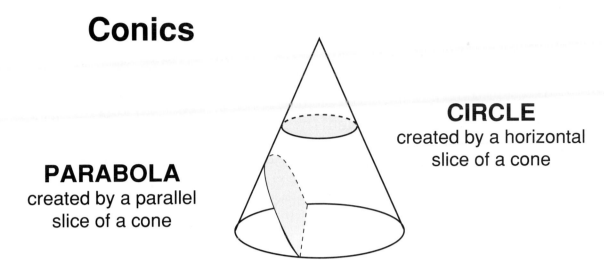

PARABOLA
created by a parallel
slice of a cone

CIRCLE
created by a horizontal
slice of a cone

Fig. 11-2

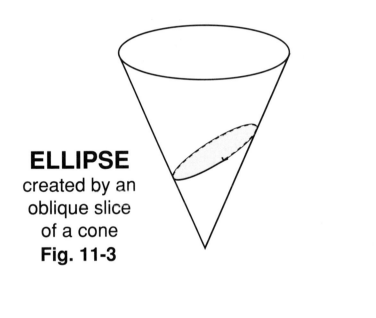

ELLIPSE
created by an
oblique slice
of a cone
Fig. 11-3

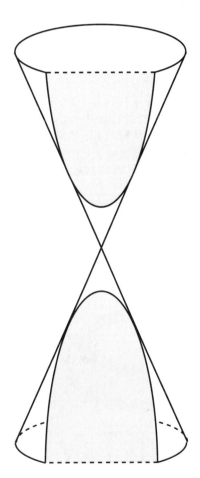

HYPERBOLA
created by a vertical
slice of a double cone
Fig. 11-4

Rotation of a simple geometric element is the most common geometric transformation used in generating a line design. Chapter 9 is devoted entirely to designs generated by rotation. Most frequently the design results in the curve illusion of a circle. As an element is rotated about a point in the plane, the corresponding parts of that element remain a constant distance from the point of rotation. A circle is defined as a curve all of whose points lie a given distance from a given point in a plane.

Figures 11-7 through 11-10 show an interesting relationship between a circle and an ellipse. If, from a point inside a circle, rays are drawn to the circle and then angles of a given measure are drawn at the point where the ray and circle intersect, an ellipse is created by the sides of the angle. Figure 11-7 shows right angles forming the ellipse. In figure 11-8, right angles are also drawn, but the point from which the rays are drawn is closer to the center of the circle. This results in a shape that is more nearly the shape of the circle.

Figures 11-9 and 11-10 show angles of 60° and 30° inscribed in the circle. It appears as though an ellipse will be formed in each case in this procedure. It also appears that the smaller the angle, the smaller the ellipse. The point from which the rays are drawn also affects the line design shape.

Previous chapters show several circular line designs such as the one in figure 11-11. Figure 11-12 reveals that the line design curve illusion is not a true circle.

Circles Made with
Line Segments

Each point on a circle
lies the same distance
from a point within.

Fig. 11-5

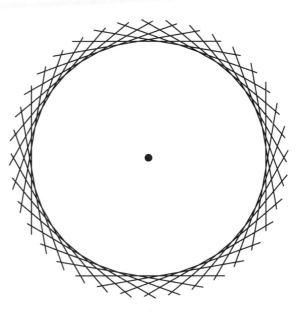

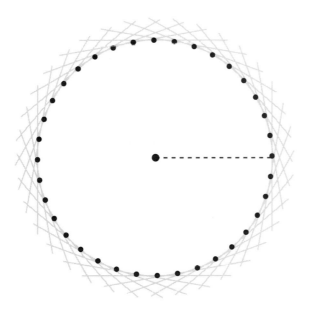

The distance from a point to
a line is the perpendicular
from the point to the line.

Fig. 11-6

Selected Angle
Inscriptions Within a Circle

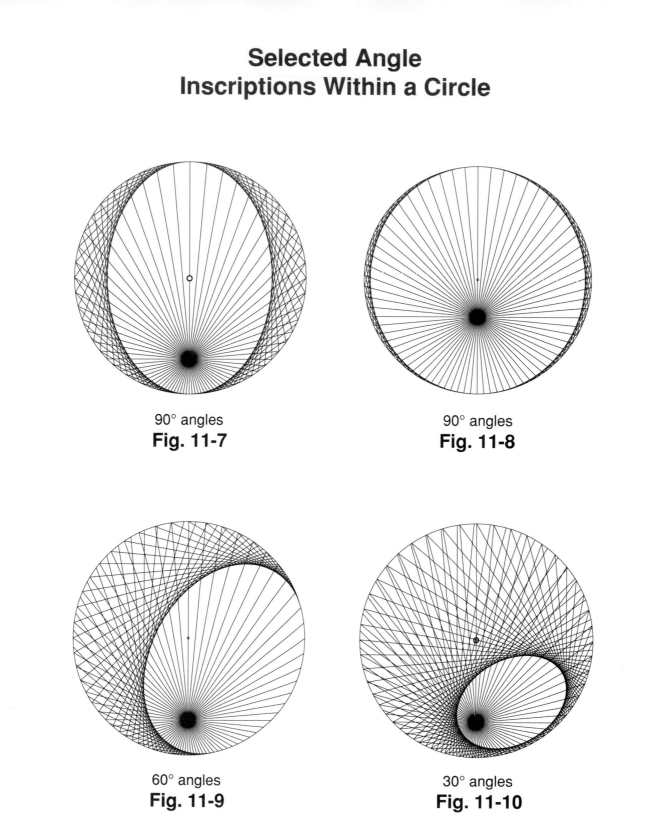

90° angles
Fig. 11-7

90° angles
Fig. 11-8

60° angles
Fig. 11-9

30° angles
Fig. 11-10

Circle-Like Curves
made with
line segments

Four 90° angle line designs
give the appearance
of a circle.
Fig. 11-11

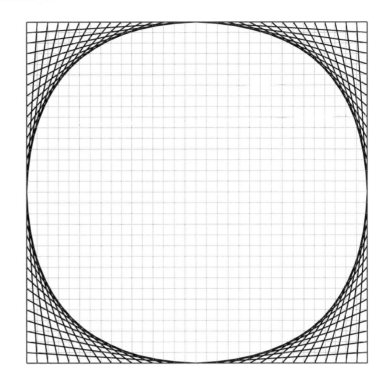

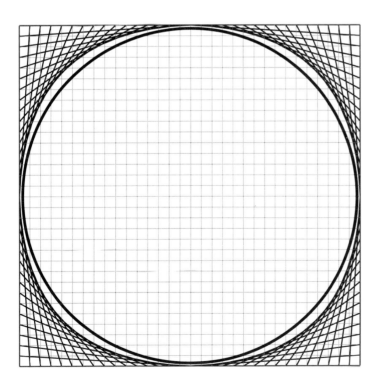

Actual circle shown reveals that
the line design is not a true circle.
Fig. 11-12

Parabolas form the most common line design curve illusions. The parabola on the top of the opposite page was formed by reflecting rays from a point off a line at right angles.

One can think of a parabola as the location of all points in a plane that are equidistant from a given point (focus) and a given line (directrix). The illustration at the bottom of the opposite page shows three points on the parabola that lie the same distance from the focus and directrix.

A parabola, like a circle, is self-similar. That is, every parabola has the exact same shape. If a parabola seems much flatter than another, it is because you are just seeing a small fraction of the parabola near its tip where all parabolas are flat. The diagrams on page 254 show seven angles of various measures. Each of these shapes is formed by straight lines only. The curve illusion in each case has the shape of a parabola. Each of the solid heavy curves was taken from the same basic parabola.

The hyperbolic paraboloid shown on page 255 must be viewed as a three-dimensional object. Its cross sections are parabolas in one direction and hyperbolas in the other direction. Hyperbolic paraboloids are frequently seen as shapes used in designing modernistic roofs.

LINE DESIGNS

Parabola
made with
line designs

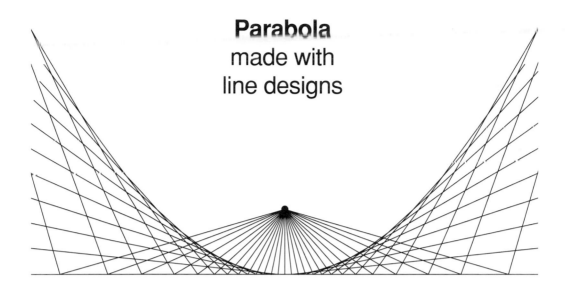

Each point on the parabola is the same distance from a given point (focus) and a given line (directrix).

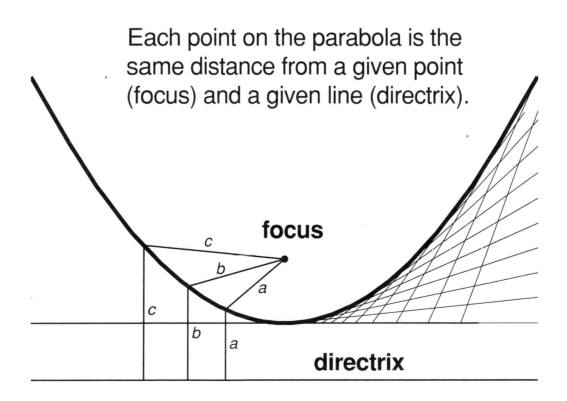

focus

c

b

a

c

b

a

directrix

Line Designs in Angles Showing Relationship to Parabolic Curves

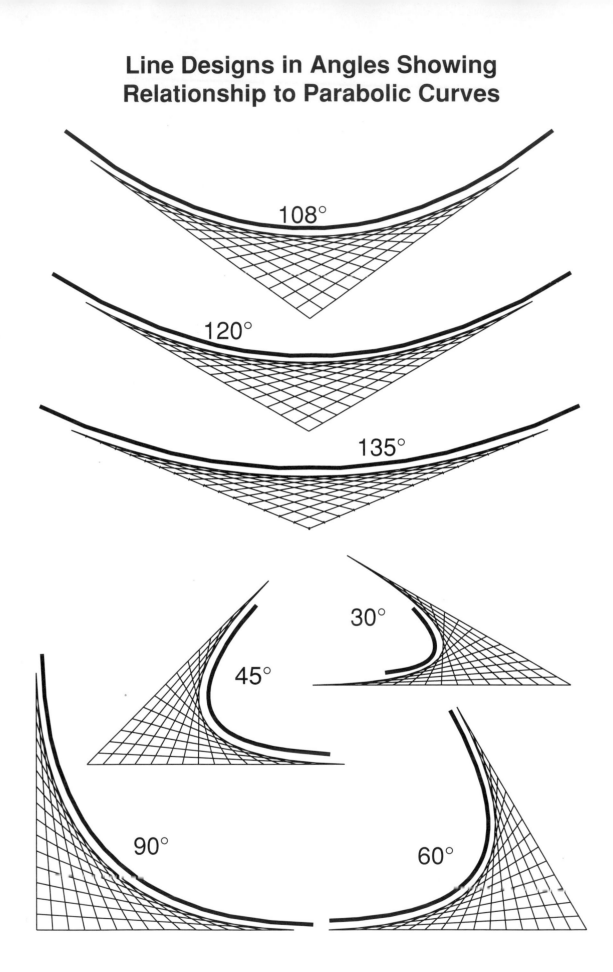

Hyperbolic Paraboloid

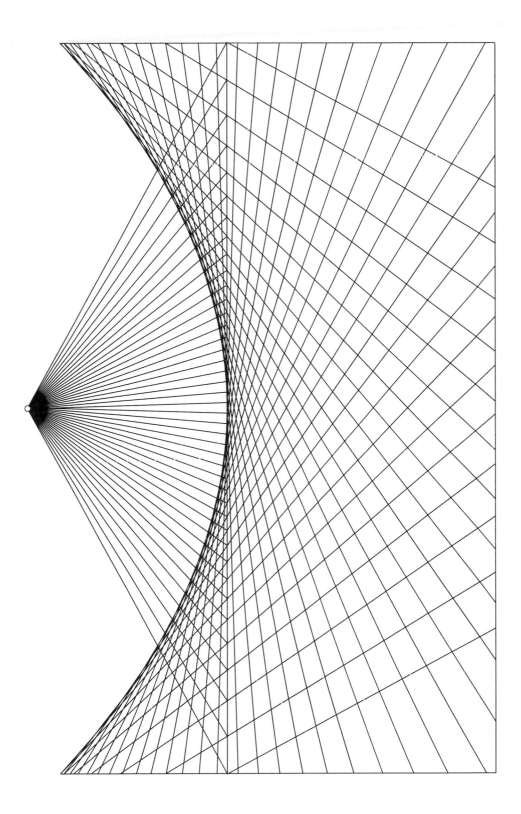

An *ellipse* may be defined as the location of all points the sum of whose distances from two fixed points is constant. In the Fig. 11-14, below, the sum $a + a'$ is equal to the sum $b + b'$. Circles and parabolas are self-similar, but ellipses can have an infinite number of different shapes.

The diagrams on the opposite page show angles of various measures inscribed in an ellipse. One side of each angle passes through the center of the figure. A describable pattern emerges. This is just one example of a number of pattern explorations that might be performed on geometric shapes. We see why mathematics is often called *the study of pattern*.

Pages 258 and 259 show line designs as elliptical shapes formed by angles inscribed in circles.

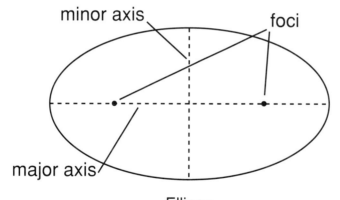

Ellipse
Fig. 11-13

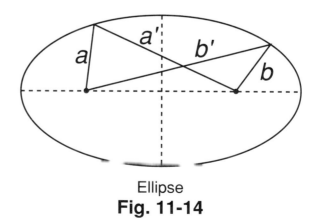

Ellipse
Fig. 11-14

Selected Angle Inscriptions
Within an Ellipse

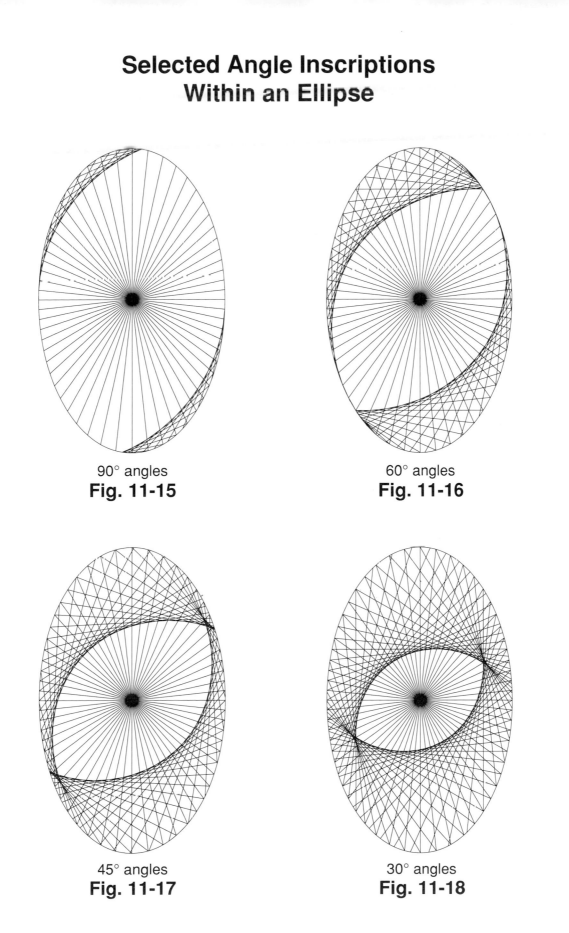

90° angles
Fig. 11-15

60° angles
Fig. 11-16

45° angles
Fig. 11-17

30° angles
Fig. 11-18

Single Elliptical Envelope
90° Inscribed Angles

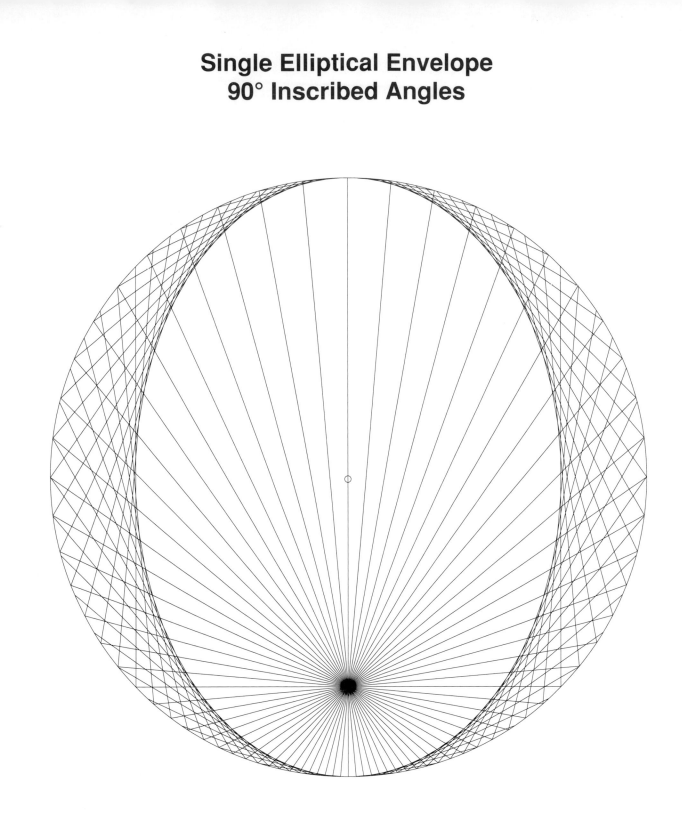

Double Elliptical Envelope
60° Inscribed Angles

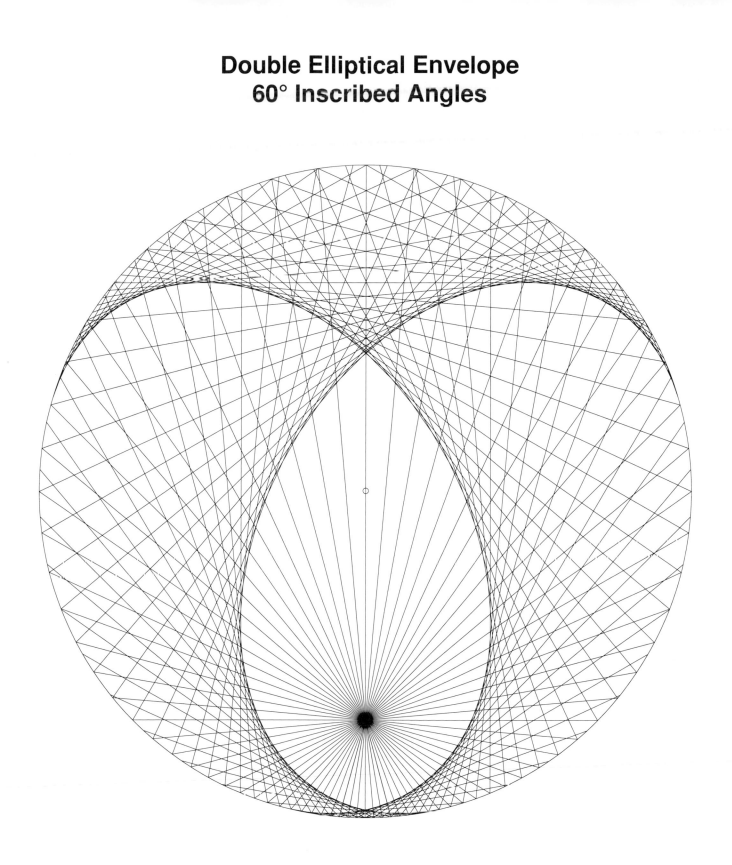

The final conic, the *hyperbola*, is defined as the location of all points for which the difference of their distances from two fixed points (the foci) is constant. The two curves have reflective symmetry about each of their axes.

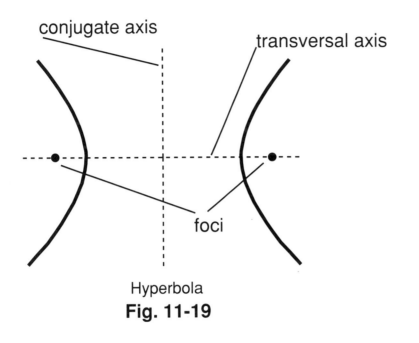

conjugate axis

transversal axis

foci

Hyperbola

Fig. 11-19

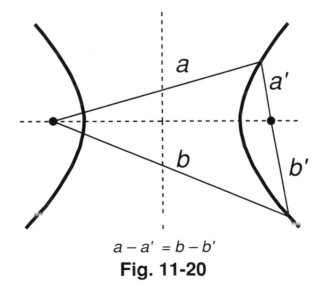

a

a'

b

b'

$a - a' = b - b'$

Fig. 11-20

Hyperbola
made with
line designs

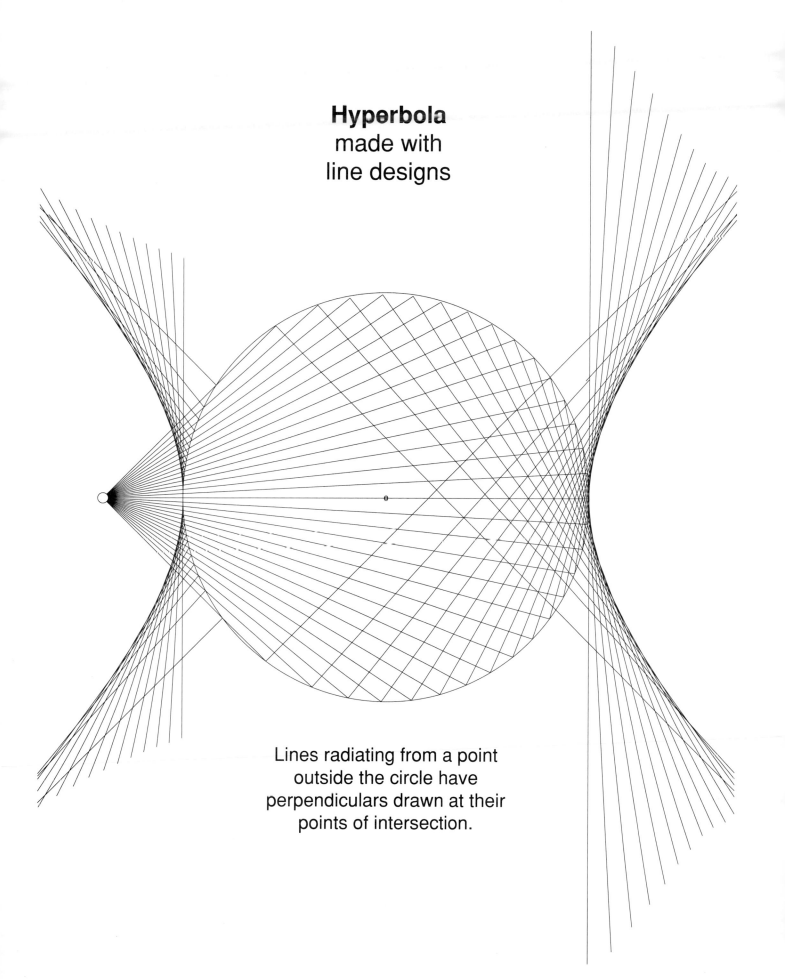

Lines radiating from a point
outside the circle have
perpendiculars drawn at their
points of intersection.

There are many interesting curves that can be generated by line-design patterns. Space limitations have required that a select few curves be presented in this book. One final, interesting curve shown on the opposite page is the *cardioid*. The cardioid is one of a family of curves known as *epicycloids*. The cardioid is a symmetrical, heart-shaped figure that can be generated by connecting selected equal division points on a circle. First the circle is divided into an equal number of arcs. Then chords are drawn to connect points 1 to 2, 2 to 4, 3 to 6, 4 to 8, etc.

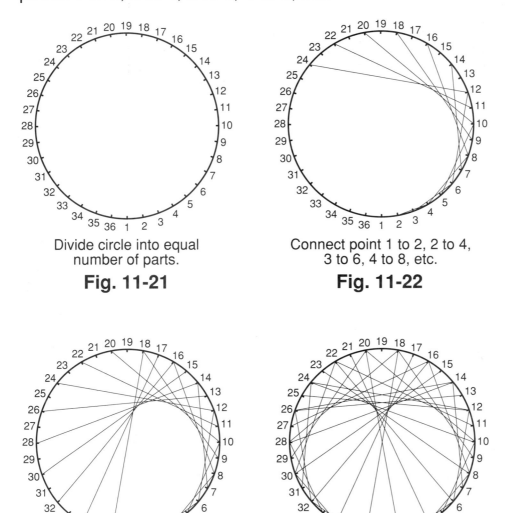

Divide circle into equal
number of parts.

Fig. 11-21

Connect point 1 to 2, 2 to 4,
3 to 6, 4 to 8, etc.

Fig. 11-22

Continue connecting
pattern halfway around.

Fig. 11-23

Connect points the same
way in the opposite direction.

Fig. 11-24

Cardioid
made with
line designs

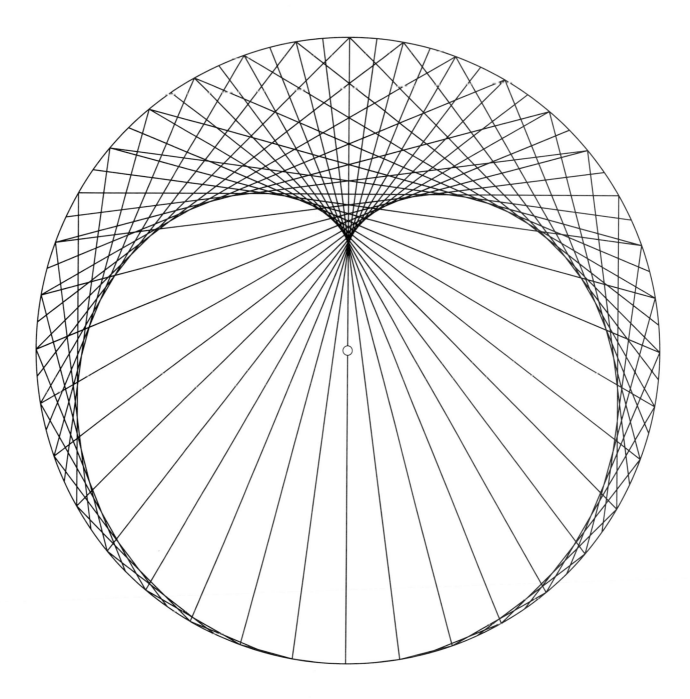

The drawings below can be thought of as sets of parallel elastic strings that are attached to two sticks (dark lines). The two sticks can be moved in any direction, thereby creating different effects.

Figures 11-27 and 11-28 show the sticks rotated in space to positions that create the line design curve illusions. The design on the opposite page was created in this manner.

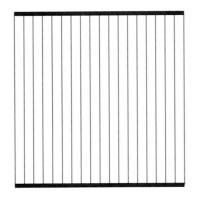

Two sticks connected at equal intervals with elastic strings

Fig. 11-25

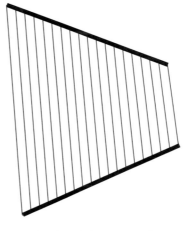

Both sticks moved to nonhorizontal positions

Fig. 11-26

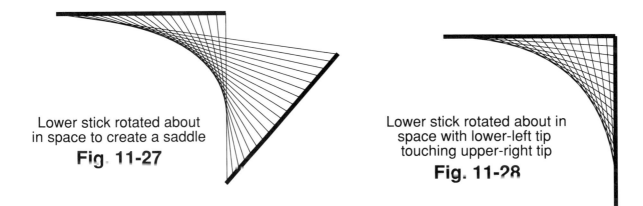

Lower stick rotated about in space to create a saddle

Fig. 11-27

Lower stick rotated about in space with lower-left tip touching upper-right tip

Fig. 11-28

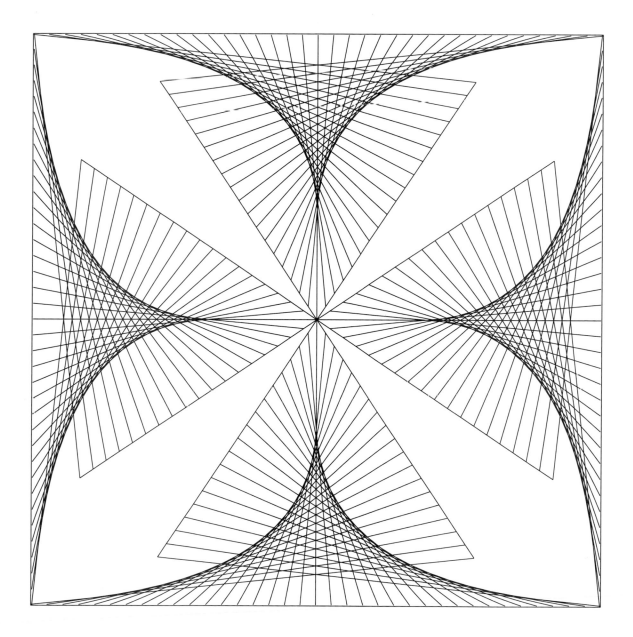

A *curve of pursuit* creates a line design curve. If we suppose that a dog sees a rabbit and takes chase, then the situation provides us with an interesting model of a curve of pursuit. The rabbit moves in a straight line towards its home (hole in the ground). The dog moves straight at the rabbit.

After a short period, the dog sees that it is not, in fact, heading directly at the rabbit (the rabbit has moved), so the dog modifies its course. This new course of the dog's is one heading directly at the rabbit again. New courses are taken by the dog at equal intervals along the chase. The dog's path in the chase is called the *curve of pursuit*. In the diagram below, it is assumed that the dog and the rabbit are traveling at the same speed.

The illustrations on the opposite page show the chase in its various stages.

Curve of pursuit
Fig. 11-29

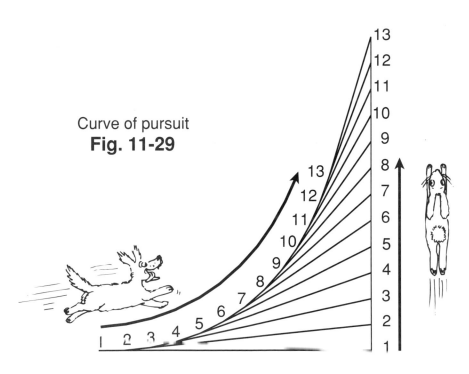

Curve of Pursuit
Dog Chasing Rabbit

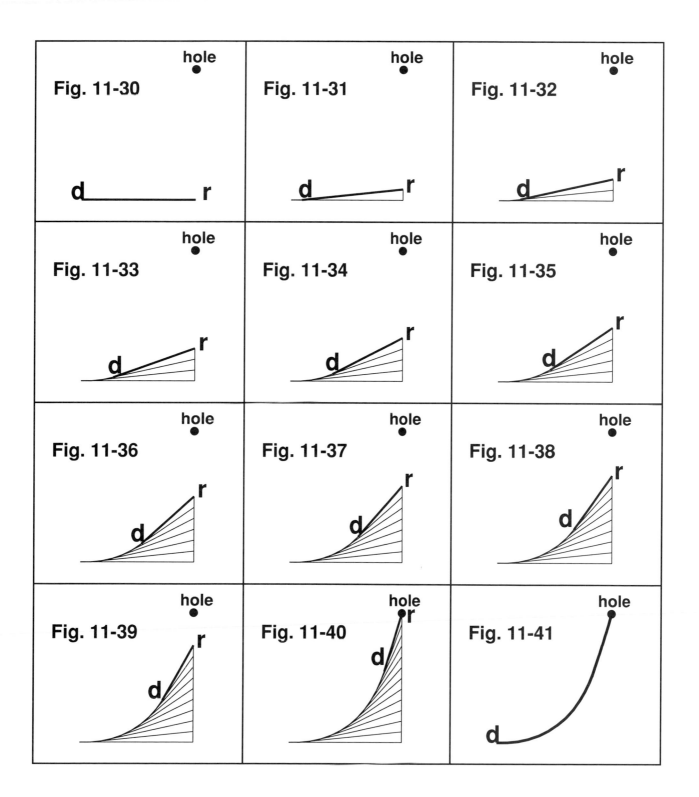

CHAPTER **12**
MOIRÉ PATTERNS

A broad definition of line designs might include some moiré patterns. *Moiré patterns* usually contain an illusion of curves created by combining geometric elements. A moiré pattern is created when one repetitive geometric design is superimposed upon another. We see moiré patterns in our world in nylon curtains, screen doors, bridge railings, waves in water, and many other places.

Moiré patterns have several useful applications in science and technology. One such example is when metals are studied for stress analysis by superimposing one photo of the metal upon another and viewing for moiré patterns. The degree of flatness of a surface can be determined by the moiré technique.

In this chapter, a few examples of moiré are shown. Most of the curve illusions are in the form of hyperbolas. Factors such as line width and space width can affect the moiré patterns. Readers who would like to study moiré patterns in more depth may wish to read the suggested references in the bibliography.

Transparency masters of some of the basic geometric patterns are furnished at the end of this chapter. These pages can be copied on transparent sheets on most photocopy machines. Combinations of two or more transparencies will produce interesting effects.

LINE DESIGNS

Concentric Circles

Concentric circles
Fig. 12-1

Fig. 12-2

Fig. 12-3

Fig. 12-4

Fig. 12-5

Fig. 12-6

Rays

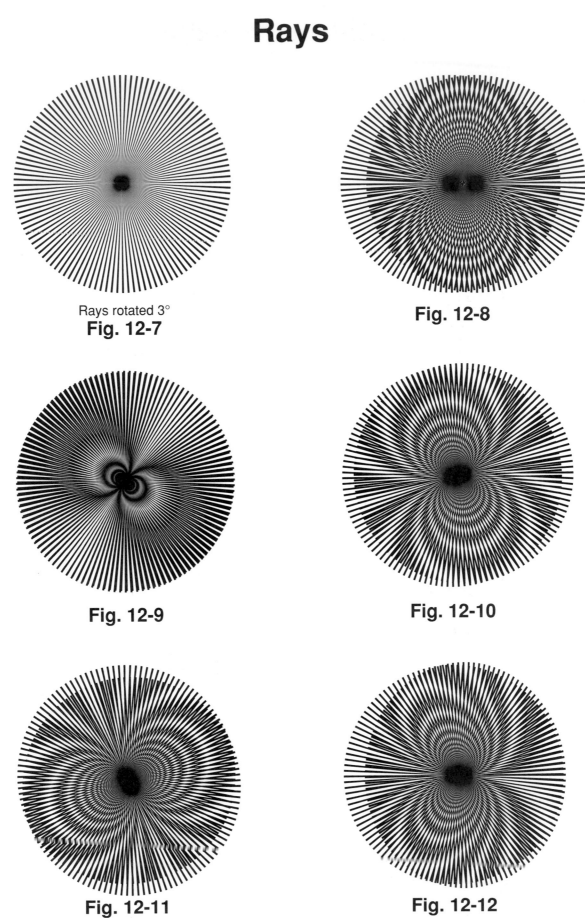

Rays rotated 3°
Fig. 12-7

Fig. 12-8

Fig. 12-9

Fig. 12-10

Fig. 12-11

Fig. 12-12

Circles and Rays

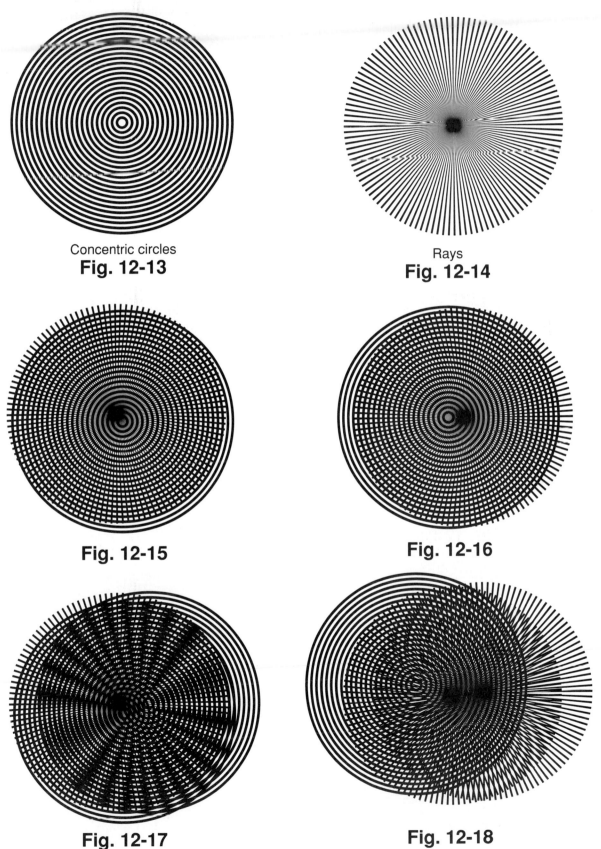

Concentric circles
Fig. 12-13

Rays
Fig. 12-14

Fig. 12-15

Fig. 12-16

Fig. 12-17

Fig. 12-18

Parallels and Circles

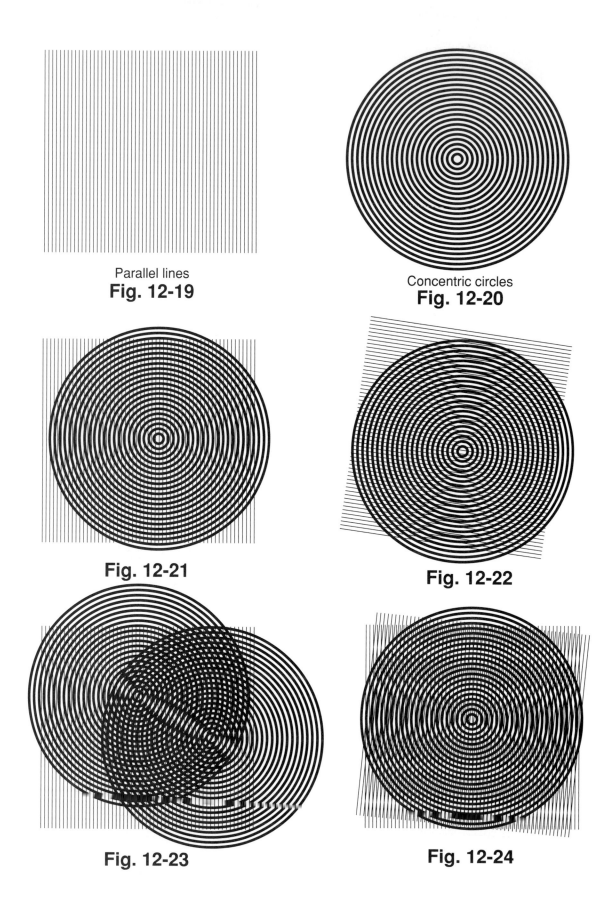

Parallel lines
Fig. 12-19

Concentric circles
Fig. 12-20

Fig. 12-21

Fig. 12-22

Fig. 12-23

Fig. 12-24

Rays and Parallels

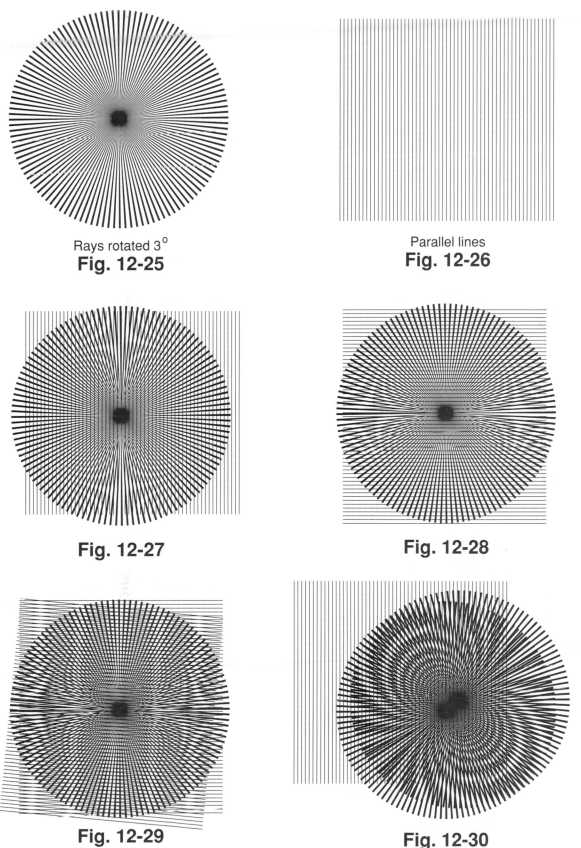

Rays rotated 3°
Fig. 12-25

Parallel lines
Fig. 12-26

Fig. 12-27

Fig. 12-28

Fig. 12-29

Fig. 12-30

Parallel Lines

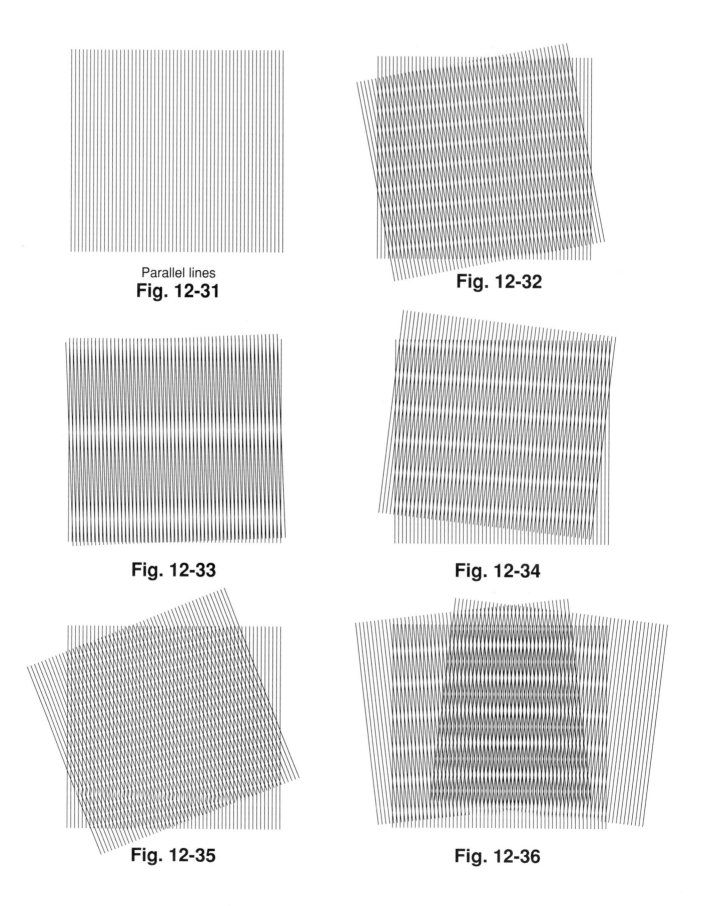

Parallel lines
Fig. 12-31

Fig. 12-32

Fig. 12-33

Fig. 12-34

Fig. 12-35

Fig. 12-36

Wavy Lines

Wavy lines
Fig. 12-37

Fig. 12-38

Fig. 12-39

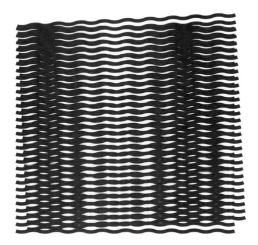

Fig. 12-40

Fig. 12-41

Fig. 12-42

Wavy and Parallel Lines

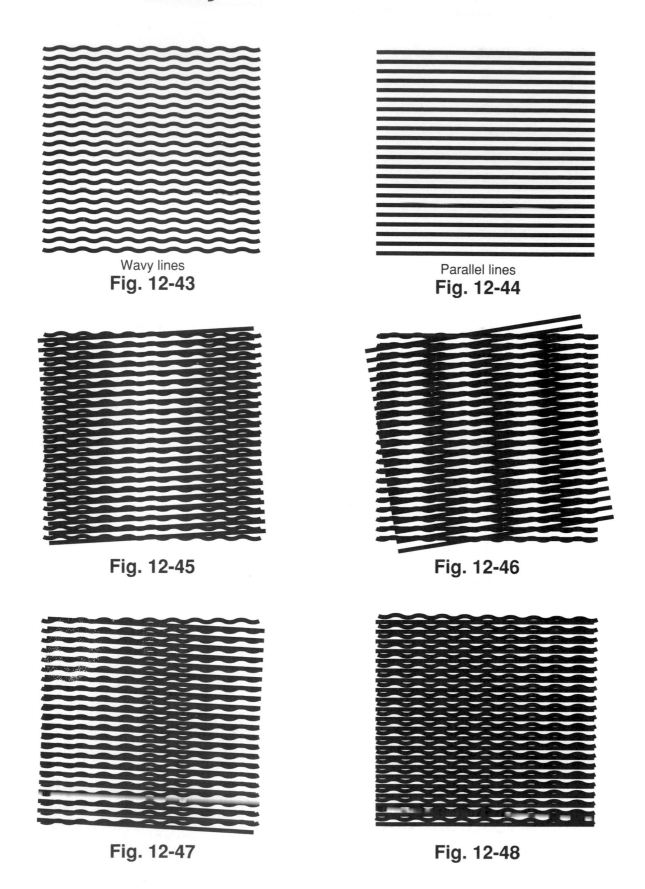

Wavy lines
Fig. 12-43

Parallel lines
Fig. 12-44

Fig. 12-45

Fig. 12-46

Fig. 12-47

Fig. 12-48

Wavy Lines, Circles, and Rays

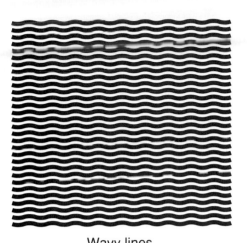

Wavy lines
Fig. 12-49

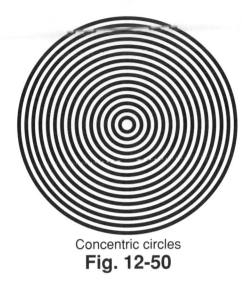

Concentric circles
Fig. 12-50

Rays
Fig. 12-51

Fig. 12-52

Fig. 12-53

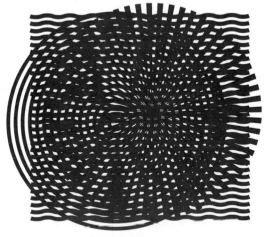

Fig. 12-54

Square and Isometric Grids

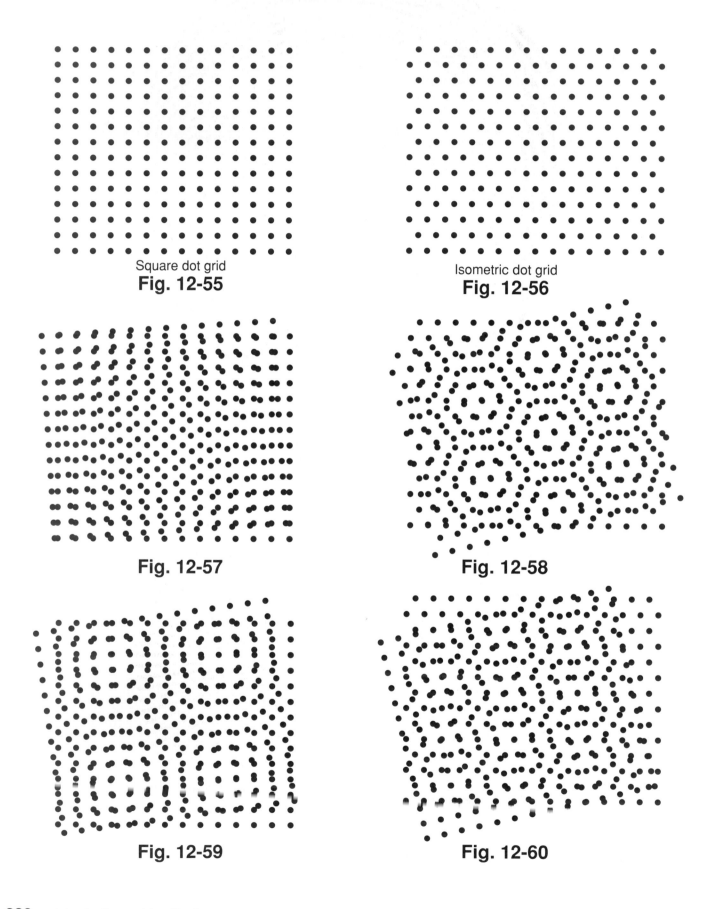

Square dot grid
Fig. 12-55

Isometric dot grid
Fig. 12-56

Fig. 12-57

Fig. 12-58

Fig. 12-59

Fig. 12-60

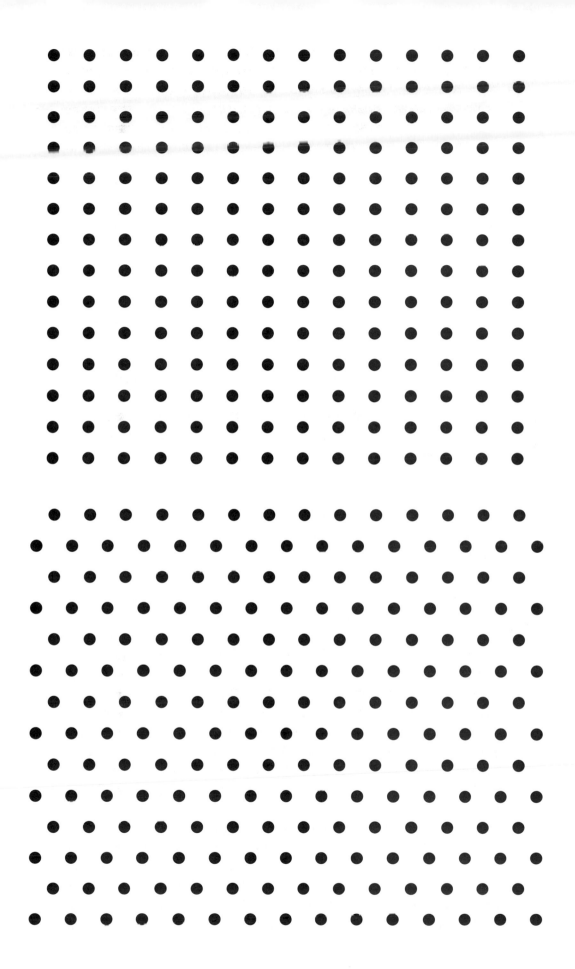

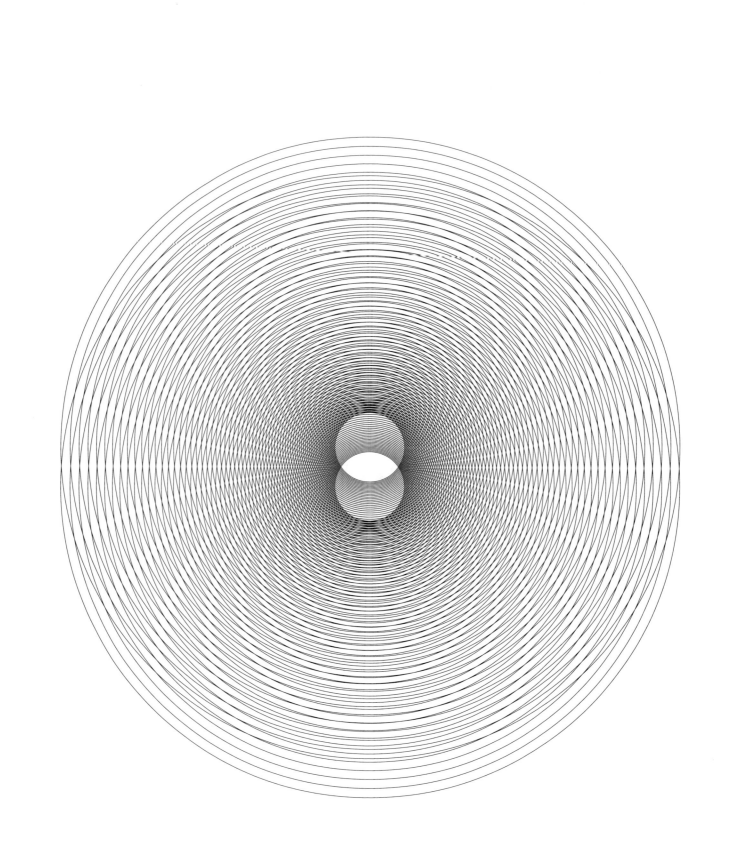

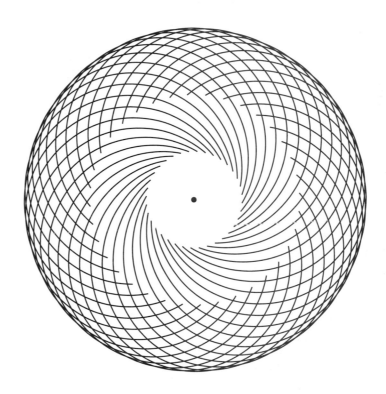

LINE DESIGN

BIBLIOGRAPHY

Cundy, H. M., and A. P. Rollett. *Mathematical Models*. New York: Oxford University Press, 1977.

An excellent general resource for information on all types of geometric models and shapes. Presents mathematical foundations for line design curves. Grades 8 to adult. 280 pp.

Line Design Poster Sets. Palo Alto, Calif.: Dale Seymour Publications, 1992.

Beautiful geometric designs created with simple straight lines, although the eye sees a series of graceful curves. Two sets available with four posters per set.

Lockwood, E. H. *A Book of Curves*. New York: Cambridge University Press, 1961.

An comprehensive treatise on plane curves. Presents formulas and basic properties of the most frequently defined curves. Grades 10 to adult. 198 pp.

Millington, J. *Curve Stitching*. Norfolk, England: Tarquin Publications, 1989.

Contains numerous colored illustrations of geometric thread art. Detailed instructions for each design include formulas and computer programs for generating the designs. Grades 6 to adult. 96 pp.

Mottershead, L. *Metamorphosis*. Palo Alto, Calif.: Dale Seymour Publications, 1977.

Contains enrichment activities on many mathematical topics, including line designs and curves of pursuit. Special emphasis on geometry and art connections. Grades 7 to adult. 192 pp.

Pohl, V. *How To Enrich Geometry Using String Designs* Reston, Va.: NCTM, 1986.

A "how-to" activities book showing the construction of several 2- and 3-dimensional string designs. Each activity is explicitly described. The book is heavily illustrated. Grades 8 to adult. 68 pp.

Seymour, D., and R. Schadler. *Creative Constructions*. Palo Alto, Calif.: Creative Publications, 1974.
> A collection of more than 250 geometric designs that can be constructed with a straightedge and compass. Includes detailed explanations of constructing six common regular polygons. Grades 6 to adult. 62 pp.

Seymour, D. *Geometric Design*. Palo Alto, Calif.: Dale Seymour Publications, 1988.
> A visual presentation of step-by-step construction of more than 80 designs based on triangles, hexagons, squares, octagons, pentagons, and decagons. Includes polygonal templates and masters for sketching original designs. Grades 6 to adult. 136 pp.

Seymour, D. *Line Designs*. Palo Alto, Calif.: Creative Publications 1974.
> A book on the techniques of creating line designs. Most geometric designs are based on inscribed polygons. Includes the basic geometric constructions. Grades 6 to adult. 80 pp.

Somervell, E. L. *A Rhythmic Approach to Mathematics*. Reston, Va.: NCTM, 1975.
> A reprint of the classic 1906 edition published by G. Philip of London. Includes the full-color plates that appeared in the original printing. Hardback. Grades 7 to adult. 72 pp.

Moiré Pattern References

Armstrong, T. *Make Moving Patterns*. Norfolk, England: Tarquin Publications, 1982.
> A full-color book-kit for making a wide variety of optical illusions and moiré patterns. Patterns are designed to be cut out to create both 2- and 3-dimensional illusions. Grades 7 to adult. 56 pp.

Encyclopedia of Science and Technology. New York: McGraw-Hill, 1987.
> Definitions, history, descriptions, and applications of moiré patterns. (See pp. 299-301.)

LINE DESIGNS

Grafton, C. B. *Optical Designs in Motion with Moiré Overlays.* New York: Dover Publications, 1976.
More than 50 different optical-art patterns to be used with four acetate optical designs. The acetates are designed to be placed over each of the printed patterns. Hundreds of design permutations. No written copy. Grades 6 to adult. 32 pp.

Moiré Array.   Hagerstown, Md.: Tedco, Inc., 1986.
Small kit of various moire pattern overlays. Overlays and designs measure 2 1/2″ x 2 1/2″. Single instruction sheet. Available through Edmund Scientific Co. Grades 7 to adult.

Oster, G., and Y. Nishijima.   "Moiré Patterns." *Scientific American,* May 1963, pp. 54-63.
Extensive article on moiré patterns. Explains origin of term *moiré;* gives applications and techniques for creation. Grades 9 to adult.